The Ultimate Medical Student Handbook

Authors

Nicholas Kalekas, DO

Daliah Wachs MD, FAAFP

_____

Dedicated to all the students who were our colleagues, then became our friends and are now family…….

_____

Table of Contents

Introduction

Let's face it. Medical school is not easy. Between the anatomy, the chemistry, the microbes, the medications, the math... you're swimming in a never ending sea of texts and graphics. And then during clinicals, you're faced with applying all that you previously learned to tons of new information, all while you are face to face with a patient who is asking, "Can you tell me what's wrong with me?"

You turn to your family for support and they give you encouragement with a, "Don't worry, no one expects you to get it right the first time... You're a student!"

But you know that's not the case. Getting it "wrong" could mean life or death. True, there is always someone more experienced around you, but mistakes can still be made and you fear you will never overcome if one happens on your watch.

And then what if you don't speak the patient's language? Will you miss key symptoms if you or the interpreter fails to capture the essence of what the patient is saying?

So it's no wonder medical school can be one of the most daunting and stressful times in one's career.

And what stands between the student and becoming a physician? Written exams and standardized patient encounters. These examinations can be tricky, as they test on many disciplines. They are designed to make you think, deduce, treat... all while ensuring you demonstrate interpersonal skills.

So you need to be the whole package. Is it doable? Is it possible to succeed? Of course! We did... but it took practice, patience and perseverance.

This *Handbook* is one of the most comprehensive books available as it helps you determine what kind of medical student personality you have. Then it walks you through the components necessary to have strong and successful patient interactions. This will not only help you pass your practice patient encounters in schooling but also help you gain fluency in skills necessary to pass written exams. We will not cite specific tests as the purpose of this *Handbook* is to assist you anywhere along your medical school training. Moreover this *Handbook* provides tips on how to study and do well on your rotations, plus prepare your personal statement for residency. You'll get great advice on how to prepare for your residency interview, plus we also include a comprehensive chapter on Medical Spanish that can help you gain some fluency while interviewing and examining the Spanish-speaking only patient.

This *Handbook* is written with both an MD and DO's perspective to give you as much insight as possible to the challenges faced during medical school training. Hopefully this eases your path a bit. Remember we got through it and made it to the other side. Here's how…...

Chapter 1   What is Humanism

Students and physicians were once regarded as stoic, insensitive, and condescending. As medicine evolved, so did the need for improved communication between providers and patients.

Antibiotics, cathartics and prescribed remedies needed to be explained. Consent became mandatory before surgery was performed. Information from non medical sources such as the internet appeared to make more of an impact on patients than "doctor's orders." Moreover as more medical professionals entered the field, competition ensued to attract patients to one's practice.

So we soon learned that if we wanted to have a successful practice and interaction with our patients, we needed to learn how to communicate with them. But in order to attract a patient, gain their trust, and capture their attention, we needed to display our humanistic side.

But how as students can we show this side if we're exhausted from studying 8-16 hours a day and trying to remember facts learned months ago? Bedside manner may unwittingly take a back seat. No matter how friendly you are, when you're faced with a difficult challenge of taking a history, assessing a condition, calculating an IV drip rate, and determining standing orders...it's really easy to forget a simple smile.

What is "humanism?"

In medicine it's a metric of one's professionalism, empathy and interpersonal relationships between patients and the healthcare team.

You can't memorize the skills like we do in anatomy, but you aren't always born with it either. Becoming empathetic requires patience and an appreciation of how your patient may feel.

Many students struggle with humanism, not because they lack people skills, but because they think they're "not good enough" to warrant a patient's attention, or because they do not yet understand what the patient has been through to get to this point. They want to avoid looking like a "cocky doctor." But connecting and engaging with a patient is easier than it looks.

So how do we connect to people?

Easy....we use the 3 E's...... Engage, Educate and Enlist.

To Engage, Educate, and Enlist works in any scenario. Whether you're a physician, nurse, spouse, parent, marketing executive, debate participant, show host, or even clergy.....we need to **engage** our audience, then **educate** them on our topic, and then **enlist** them to take action.

In anything we do, we need to connect with whom we're speaking

If we connect, we can establish rapport

If we establish rapport, we establish trust.

If we establish trust, they will receive our education.

Once educated, we can enlist them to follow requests, i.e. follow a diet, fill a prescription, make a follow up appointment, etc.

For example. Lets say a patient presents with rectal bleed and has a family history of colon cancer. But the patient already told the nurse he will "never have a colonoscopy!!" due to the perceived embarrassment of the procedure. The doctor now has the challenging task of convincing the patient to be evaluated by a specialist. So he may choose to do the following:

Engage: *I had a colonoscopy as well. Wasn't excited about the idea of a camera inside my colon, or having to undress for the procedure......*

Educate: *But it was easier than I thought. And there are no other procedures that look at the inside of you colon, can biopsy, and be painless (if sedated) all at the same time such as a colonoscopy to look at your problem. I also learned it is one of the simplest life saving procedures you can get done for yourself.*

Enlist: *So at least meet and sit down with the gastroenterologist and discuss the procedure in detail so you can get your concerns addressed.*

So if we properly engage a patient, they will be open to our education and then our suggestions.

So in medicine how do we accomplish this?

Engagement

Engagement begins immediately upon entering the room.

The *Greeting* is your first opportunity to command attention and therefore engage the patient.

So make eye contact, shake their hand, thank them for waiting, be sincere and address them with respect.

If there are ethnic barriers prohibiting you from greeting with a hand shake, a gentle touch on the shoulder, or nod with head in respect can do.

Then identify yourself – you want them to remember you and engage with you.

Ex. "I'm Student Dr. Smith."
Explain why you are there. *"I'm here to help you today."*
Inquire as to what they want. *"What would you like to discuss?"* or *"How can I help you?"*

Engagement tips to be discussed later in this book include:
> Washing hands in front of the patient
> Making small talk while washing the hands
> Shaking their hand once your hand is dry
> Asking if they are comfortable
> Asking permission to sit
> Position chair so the patient doesn't have to turn to look at you
> Lean forward and make eye contact
> Reflectively listen
> Offer a tissue if they are crying
> Stand up and look at where they are pointing if referring to a painful body part

Offering a drape if they are cold or exposed

Giving positive feedback when they say they stick to a good diet, or avoid tobacco

Education

Assuming you engaged the patient well and performed a proper H&P or Subjective/Objective part to your SOAP note you will have the valuable opportunity of sitting back down in front of the patient and having their full attention.

Now is the time to *Educate*.

First, ask what they understand about their symptoms/condition and what they feel could be going on. Secondly, use easy to understand language when explaining. Thirdly, make sure they understand what you are telling them as you explain. Inquire if they are clear on what you have said.

Now some of us may feel pressured to give a diagnosis right away. DO NOT diagnose without all the data needed to make an appropriate diagnosis. That's what differentials are for. For example, if someone is having chest pain but you aren't convinced it's a heart attack as they are coughing and producing sputum then you can say that. "Your *Chest Pain* could be caused by a variety of issues such as bronchitis and costochondritis but we will rule out heart attack as well."

If the patient demands certainty, share with them your knowledge and what you need to make a conclusive decision.

"If you are concerned about appendicitis, we will know more once we receive your lab tests and CT result."

Or one can say the following: *"I'm going to discuss your case with my attending and will return to speak with you about our plan."*

Then we need to offer immediate education once we receive more data as patients don't want to be kept in the dark.

"Once I learn of your results we will contact you." ▪

Then have the patient repeat back what they have learned, or ask if they understand their diagnosis.

"So what did you learn today?"

Enlisting

The patient by now has been engaged and educated, but your job is not done.

Now you need to ensure your objectives are met and enlist them to perform what is needed.

These may include recommendations to:

- Leave a urine sample
- Have a colonoscopy
- Make the referral appointment
- Fill the prescription
- Follow up in two weeks

Of course this is performed with utmost sensitivity to:

- their needs
- constraints of time
- finances
- transportation
- work commitments
- personal preferences (shot vs oral, flavors of medication)

So an example of *enlisting* would be:

"Now that you understand why maintaining your blood sugar is so important with your diagnosis of diabetes, I'd like you to check your blood sugars with the glucometer, log them down, and bring them with you to your next visit with me. When can you see me next?"

So you see, if you engage the patient, educate them, and enlist them, you will have a successful encounter.

Chapter 2 What are Objective Structured Clinical Examinations (OSCE's) and What do these Standardized Tests Look For?

One of the best strategies we've always found when taking a test is knowing the tester's objectives. When a student is being tested on how he interacts with a patient and deduces their differential diagnosis, you can bet real money (and you do with the cost of the test) that they will test you on multiple cases, use a variety, make sure they hit some common conditions, and then see how you do when the answer is not so obvious.

You're being tested on competency but also professionalism. If you don't know the answer, they will observe how you react. We'll explain later what to do in that situation.

The Standardized Patients (SP's)

It is the job of the healthcare professional to be humanistic towards the patient. However, because medical students take standardized OSCE exams in order to practice their humanism skills, we introduce the question, "How does one measure humanism and assign a grade to it?" It is because of this dilemma that we assume standardized patients will be scripted and act semi-conservatively in order to not introduce too much variability during a graded encounter. Therefore, we would like to call this our "robot theory" as to how you might expect standardized OSCE patients to behave.

During a practice case or exam the students expect the SP's to act like actual patients, i.e. engaging in conversations, making facial expressions, nodding in agreement, etc. However, to their surprise, they find a "robot." Remember they were hired to be a patient in a specific case. When one is hired to perform as an actor, they are given a script. Rarely are actors allowed to go "off script" especially in a standardized test setting in medical school. So you probably shouldn't expect them to carry on conversations or answer remote questions fluently without being prompted to do so. Although this may be intimidating and discouraging, it can actually work towards your advantage.

If an SP seems robotic along one line of questioning and then lights up when you come across a specific line of questioning, this may mean you're on the right track. However, if they never light up, don't let that dissuade you either. If you used a broad differential or your columns (explained later in this book) and got "nothing" from them, take a deep breath and move on to the physical. It is also possible that they are meant to respond "no" to every ROS question, in which case they might not have any particular diagnosis, but rather, they are simply testing your ability to ask about a wide range of ROS questions and include many differential diagnoses. In other words, they might deny everything just to see how you think, respond, and handle the situation.

But don't panic if your standardized patient is quiet or non talkative...that's what robots do.

In the coming chapters real life patients will be referred to as "patients" and standardized patients will be referred to as "robots."

Chapter 3 What do Patients Look For

This gets tricky. In medical school, we think all patients want a doctor who is cerebral, academic, all-knowledgeable, and can answer every question with 100% accuracy. And if you poll the average patient they will believe they want that too. But which doctors seem to attract the most patients and *keep* them? The answer isn't so simple.

It depends on the mood, condition, and healthcare access a patient has.

The Scared Patient

If a patient is scared that their condition could be serious or carry a poor prognosis, they're going to want the facts and not a lot of "chit chat". Students find these cases challenging as they were trained that "chit chat" can increase humanism in the encounter. However, in these cases the "chit- chat" will come after the news.

So how do we break the news? Depends on the patient. Some may want the facts matter-of-factly:

"We think your weight loss may be due to colon cancer."

And some may want the news given smoothly:

"There may be many reasons for your weight loss ranging from malabsorption, to a hypermetabolic state caused by your thyroid or possibly a mass in your colon."

Either route must, however, be followed by an immediate plan. However, allow enough time for the differential to sink in.

"We think your weight loss may be due to colon cancer......so if you're willing, I'd like to refer you to a gastroenterologist who can perform your colonoscopy, see what's going on, and take a biopsy if necessary."

We prefer, and so do the standardized tests, the offering of the differential with the plan for each of the potential diagnoses.

"There may be many reasons for your weight loss ranging from malabsorption, to a hypermetabolic state caused by your thyroid or possibly mass in your colon.......so in addition to blood work to check your vitamins and thyroid levels, we will refer you to a gastroenterologist who can perform your colonoscopy, see what's going on, and take a biopsy if necessary."

Many times the patient, or standardized patient will ask *"Do I have cancer?"* This is a very difficult question to answer, even for the fully graduated physician.

So the best route to take is one of complete honesty. If all testing and biopsies have confirmed cancer, you say "yes." However, if cancer is in your differential, and many times it is just a suspicion, you can answer:

"At this time it is unclear what your diagnosis is as your weight loss can be caused by a variety of causes such as malabsorption, hyperthyroid or a malignancy. This is why we will investigate all of these possibilities so we can confirm as soon as possible what is the reason for your weight loss."

The Patients Who Want Reassurance

Many patients, including standardized, want reassurance that their condition is not serious. So in a case of a patient presenting with back pain, whose father died of colon cancer, if he asks "Do you think I have cancer?" a response could be:

That's an excellent question. Are you having symptoms such as weight loss? Fatigue? Blood in the stool? Lack of appetite? Constipation? No? Well that's very reassuring, but we will still rule out colon cancer to put your mind at ease as it is in our differential.

The Patients Who Want to Be Listened To

The humanism points gained here will be based on well you *listen*. If they feel they were not rushed and truly listened to, they will appreciate you and find your humanism exemplary.

So how do you prove to them you listened?

Firstly, ask permission to take a seat and then face the patient while maintaining good eye contact. Then, allow them to answer your questions fully and continue. If they get too wordy you can always redirect, but then allow them to continue explaining.

Then, recap or summarize what they told you. This can occur after the physical when you are about to give your assessment and plan. It's a nice way to close an encounter as it demonstrates you were listening, allows you to recheck your history for accuracy, and put the history to memory moments before you write your SOAP note.

The Patients Who Want to Be Cheered Up

Don't panic in this case. No one is expecting you to be an entertainer. You are a medical professional. But the patient may be looking to you for validation that their bad breath, hemorrhoids, discharge, or erectile dysfunction does not make them a monster. Your educating them on how common some of these conditions can be and how easily they can be treated, will provide some much needed relief and make the patient feel better.

The Patients Who Want Cheerleading

Losing 5 pounds may not seem like a lot to you and still be far away from their goal of losing 60, but patients will come to see you for support and recognition. If they improved their blood sugars, or cholesterol numbers, or blood pressure readings, or quit tobacco, show some excitement, congratulate them and encourage them to keep up the great work.

The Patients Who Want Pain Medication

The idea that all patients who request pain medication are "drug seekers" is a myth. The average patient who requests pain medication is actually scared.....scared of pain, or scared of going through withdrawal. Opioid withdrawal can be extremely painful and many patients may opt to just keep taking opiates rather than face diarrhea, abdominal cramps, tremors, muscle aches, insomnia and anxiety. You'll be surprised to find many patients asking for a controlled substance are tired of being enslaved to the medication and would like to break free. Find common ground and offer them resources for help or other methods to treat their ailments.

Chapter 4 What Medical Student Personality Type are You?

A misconception in medicine is you have to be a "people person," insinuating that you must love being around people to be successful in medicine. Yet the field of medicine is vast and those who choose to dedicate their lives to pediatrics may differ greatly in personality from one who devotes their career to pathology. So every one of our personalities brings to the table certain strengths and certain weaknesses. Let's determine which personality is yours by taking the following quiz:

Circle the answer that fits you best and tally the letter of which answers you choose:

1. If I have no plans on a Saturday night, the following appeals to me the most:

      a. Watching funny videos online
      b. Stay home and read a book
      c. Do a crossword puzzle
      d. Get nervous that I was alone and lock my doors
      e. Plan my next week's schedule or catch up on work that needs to be done
      f.   Call some buddies to hang out
      g. What? I'm never without plans on a Saturday night

2. You're in line for a concert and talking to a friend. If a stranger standing behind you taps you on the shoulder and says, "Knock Knock!" What would most likely be your response:

  a. "Who's there?"
  b. Nothing I would turn around and pretend I didn't know him
  c. I would look at him and forget what my line was until he reminded me to say "who's there?"
  d. I wouldn't answer but would wonder why Knock Knock jokes ever became popular
  e. I would tell him to leave me alone and return to my conversation with my friend
  f.   I would get other people's attention in line to listen to the joke
  g. I would let him continue but then finish the joke for him

3. You're at a restaurant and pressed for time because it's your lunch hour. Your server, as she's coming to your table with food, trips and spills the plate all over your table. You most likely would:

   a. Laugh and clap, applauding her grace, putting her at ease
   b. Hide your face as the restaurant may be staring at you and the mess
   c. Nothing just watch her get up and clean the mess
   d. Wonder what she tripped on and why the projectile of the food landed effortlessly on your table
   e. Leave your seat to help her clean up asking her to just go and get another plate as you're in a hurry and you'll handle the mess
   f. Talk to her while she's cleaning up saying "oh this happens to me all the time."
   g. Look to other customers with a look of surprise as if you've never seen such clumsiness

4. A patient comes in to the clinic and asks you to evaluate him for new onset frequent expelling of gas and soiling his underwear when he does. Your next response may most likely be:

   a. Making a farting sound with both your hands in front of your mouth
   b. Change the subject quickly as you are getting embarrassed
   c. Say "um" and pause before you ask him about drug allergies
   d. Ask him to show you an example of the soiled underwear so you can quantitate the amount
   e. Say "Poop happens" and move onto the physical exam
   f. Discuss the time you had a bad bean burrito and soiled yourself as well
   g. Make a frown and say, "Hmmm...I can't imagine what that would be like!"

5. When you get nervous, you are more likely to:

   a. Make jokes
   b. Get quiet
   c. Freeze and do nothing
   d. Overthink things
   e. Acknowledge you're nervous and move onto the next task
   f. Talk to yourself until you calm down
   g. I don't get nervous

6. Which of the following statements most appeals to you:
`

   a. Find the humor in life
   b. A fool speaks while a wise man listens
   c. As long as everything goes to plan, I'm golden
   d. Think of the solution, not the problem
   e. Don't dwell on the past
   f. I can talk myself out of anything
   g. When you're right, you're right

If three or more of your answers are "a" you would fall into the category of:
   The Comedian
If three or more of your answers are "b" you would fall into the category of:
   The Shy One
If three or more of your answers are "c" you would fall into the category of:
   The Freezer
If three or more of your answers are "d" you would fall into the category of:
   The Thinker
If three or more of your answers are "e" you would fall into the category of:
   The Get-to-Businesser
If three or more of your answers are "f" you would fall into the category of:
   The Talker
If three or more of your answers are "g" you would fall into the category of:
   The Over Confident

Chapter 5 Strategy by Personality Type

Comedian

For those of us who like to make jokes, we need to stop and realize why we are doing so. Are we joking because we are nervous? Are we joking because we want the attention? Do we want validation of an audience? True your patient is an audience but they aren't there to be entertained. They are there to be listened to.

The comedian personality type, however could provide both benefits and risks. One benefit is you can put a patient at ease with a little humor. The risk, however, comes when the patient is in no mood to joke.

So err on the side of caution. When in doubt, leave it out. You and your friends may think you're funny, but someone who is worried that their ear pain may actually a brain tumor will not be in the right frame of mind to accept and laugh at a joke, making you in turn nervous when a joke fails.

Avoid making light of any issue, but be receptive to any light humor brought up by the patient. Let them be in control of the initial mood of the visit and then you can reassure them if its warranted or put them at ease if the situation allows.

The Shy One

You're shy and don't perform at your best with people. Some of your best work is when you are alone getting things done. But medicine is full of people interactions so we will have to overcome some of our shyness to succeed on a standardized exam or your clinicals.

Your strategy, then, is keeping the patient interaction simple. Rather than complex banter and conversations, you can begin with the humanistic tips taught later in this book and then "get down to business." The patient will do most of the talking and if not, and there appears to be an awkward pause... keep your script of questions (power questions taught later in this book).

Your job is to get the information, make them feel taken care off and then get out of the room... but don't look like you're in a hurry to leave. Knowing your time in the room is finite may help you.

The Freezer

You're capable, competent, but then stage fright gets the best of you. This can be the most challenging when performing a practical exam.

Those who "freeze" need a "go to" in case this happens. Your "go to" may be your SOAP note mnemonics, or bubbles/categories, or even a simple statement.

So for example, let's say you are taking one's history and during the family history the patient describes his father's death by heart attack but then asks you "can we hurry it up? Why are you asking so many questions?"

Or maybe they ask, "do you think I'm having a heart attack too?"

Surprisingly, students can easily prepare for these questions with general statements such as (for the first question), "Thank you for being patient with my history taking, it really helps us in forming your diagnosis today."

Or for the second question, "Although we cannot exclude a heart attack with certainty until testing, your informing me of your family history is very helpful in helping us decide what we need to rule out."

Most 'freezing questions" are very similar, so having an answer ready to go when asked these questions will help you "unfreeze" and then redirect to your next line of questioning.

To avoid getting lost and unable to return to your line of questioning use a template, mnemonic, or "bubbles" that help you visualize where you need to be and what still needs to be completed.

The Thinker

Some students may look like they "froze" but they are actually thinking. For some of us we can take the history and physical and conceptualize the diagnosis as we go. For others they need to get all the facts and sit down and sort through them.

But when a student begins to mentally work through a diagnosis while a patient is talking and then goes silent in thought, the dearth of conversation may seem awkward.

For those students we recommend "thinking out loud." Walk the patient through your thought process. An example would be:

"Well this chest pain could be cardiac in nature but you're not dizzy, sweating or having shortness of breath. That's good. If this chest pain was pulmonary in nature you might have wheezing, cough or phlegm……" and so on.

Points will be gained on humanism and data gathering as you are walking the patient through the differentials.

Again this may not be necessary for all student types (and it could be time consuming) but may be useful for the "thinker" or even the "freezer."

The Get-To-Businesser

Let's face it. Some of us didn't get through college and medical school by chit chatting. We hit the books and got down to business. The way we attacked our studies must have worked because now we're months away from graduating. However some of us may accidentally use this "get to business" approach during patient interactions, failing humanistically.

So you have two options. One, soften it up a little and don't seem so eager to get to the bottom of the history before they have a chance to speak. Or two, schmooze a little and then say, *"Ok now we'll get to work figuring out what's going on."* Sometimes acknowledging that you will be direct for a short period of time is softer than just always being direct.

The Talker

Chit chat is our thing. We seem to feel in control when we dominate the conversation. It's often also our go-to when we're nervous. So a nervous medical student may start talking incessantly while interviewing a patient. We may be so nervous that we interrupt the patient, losing any humanistic ground we gained earlier when we chit chatted.

Talkers need to take a deep breath and learn to listen. Patients feel like they have some control when they get to participate in the conversation. So if you become nervous during a patient encounter, ask the patient to "expand more" on the subject allowing you to stop talking, take a deep breath and regroup your thoughts. And if you feel you forgot our advice, and over spoke throughout the encounter, this is very easily remedied by saying, *"Were you able to get all your concerns addressed?"* or *"Do you have any questions for me?"*

The Over Confident

Medical school is not for the timid, so to get where you are today, you had to have confidence in yourself. Moreover, confidence is a huge factor in winning over a patient as they prefer someone who will make a decision and follow it through over someone who is indecisive.

However one thing patients hate is a cocky doctor. Being overconfident can hurt you to the point that you may never recover in that patient's eyes. So you have two options. One is to become less cocky. Could take years. So the second option is to preface what you say by directly addressing your true confidence level or using the phrase *"I am hopeful."* A person who hopes appears to be less cocky...... *"I'm fairly confident we can help relieve some of your pain."* or *"I am hopeful that after we receive your test results we will come to a conclusion on what may be causing your symptoms"*.

Chapter 6 How to Improve Your Confidence

So what if you don't have much confidence to begin with? How do you appear to a patient, who is scared, that you are in control and worthy of taking on their care?

Well many of the steps we outline in the Humanism chapter, will build confidence and professionalism. But we need to work on the inside before we dress up the outside. So let's get started.

1. Look at yourself in the mirror in your white coat. Remember the first day you tried it on as a first year medical student? It was intimidating, and although it made you smile in excitement, you worried if you could ever fit its proverbial sleeves. Well now you're deep into your training and deserve to wear the white coat more than ever. You've dressed the part, but feel it.

2. Picture a doctor you've admired and think about how they spoke with patients. Although you will develop your own "doctor personality" sometimes practicing by mimicking another helps you form a flow.

3. When in doubt, tell yourself it's OK to not know the answer. Remember every physician has multiple times in their career said *"I don't know."* You're about to be one of us so act like it. Say you don't know when you don't.

4. If you feel a patient wants to know a definitive answer, and you don't have one, be honest. Explain what you don't know and why you don't know it. *"I can't say definitively if your pain is stemming from your ovary until after we perform the pelvic ultrasound."*

5. Eat and sleep well. If you're poorly fed and exhausted, how can you stand upright and exude confidence? Make sure you feel good on the inside.

6. Be mentally fit. It's easy to become overwhelmed in school and lose yourself, so get the help you need to stay strong mentally.

7. Finally, know your stuff. With test taking, if you gain proficiency in the material being tested, you have an easier time passing the test. Same goes with patients. If you read a patient's medication list and find a drug that sounds unfamiliar, look it up. Then you can look super confident saying something like this, *"So Mrs.*

Smith, how well is the immunomodulator managing your psoriatic arthritis?" You see, you're already sounding like a doctor.

Chapter 7 The History and Physical and SOAP Note

Each time you see a patient, you are required to ask, examine and document the encounter. The two major forms of documentation are the History and Physical and the SOAP note.

The History and Physical (H & P) is taken at each new encounter with a patient. It's comprehensive and gives you a clear medical picture of the patient you are about to take care of.

This is contrast to the S.O.A.P (SOAP) note, which is done during every encounter with the patient. It is focused and summarizes the visit

SOAP stands for Subjective, Objective, Assessment, and Plan.

Subjective is what the *patient tells* the provider. This includes:

- Chief Complaint
- History of Present Illness
- Past Medical History
- Social History
- Family History
- Allergies and Medications
- Review of Systems

Objective is what the *medical provider finds*. This includes:

- Physical Exam
- Laboratory results
- Radiology results
- Emergency room/clinic treatment course
- Updates on what was done that visit
- Procedures performed

The **Assessment** is your conclusion based on the subjective and objective data.

Is it here you make your diagnosis and create a differential of medical conditions you want to rule out.

Then your **Plan**, is just that. Your plan on what you want to do. This may include:

- Tests to be run (labs, radiology)
- Medications to be prescribed
- Treatment such as OMM
- Referrals
- Work Restrictions
- Home instructions
- Follow up

SOAP notes may vary in length as some may write a whole H & P during a follow up visit if they feel they need more information, whereas others may just briefly touch upon the subjective, objective, assessment and plan necessary for their focused exam. The process, however is very similar and broken down as follows:

Chief Complaint (CC):

State what is bringing the patient in today
Should be in the patient's own words…..quotations may be used
Should be brief and focused
Should be no more than one sentence in length
Should not include a diagnosis
If no specific chief complaint is given but someone presents for a physical, you can write "Physical".

If multiple chief complaints are given by the patient, address and list first the most acute.

Example: *Patient presents today saying "I have a tummy ache"*

History of Present Illness (HPI)

This is the information surrounding the chief complaint, or as it states, the history surrounding the patient's present illness.

Institutions vary on how to preface, such as name, age, gender, gravida, race.

Ex: *Mary is a 25 year old G1P1 Hispanic female complaining of abdominal pain.......*

Now we get some more intel on the present illness such as:

Onset

> When did it start, have you had this before, what were you doing when the pain started?

Location

> Where is the pain?

Duration

> How long has it been going on?

Ex: *The pain began this morning in the right lower abdomen and has lasted 4 hours*

Severity

> Is the pain mild, moderate or severe? On a scale of 1-10 (with 10 being the worst pain imaginable) how would you rate your pain?

Radiation

> Does the pain go anywhere?

Quality

> What does the pain feel like (cramping, colicky, pressure)?

Palliative/Provocative factors

What makes the pain better/worse?

Ex: *She describes the pain as 5/10, pressure feeling, radiating to her pelvis, acetaminophen has not helped, bumps during the car ride make it worse*

OPQRST mnemonic is used very commonly to remember the components of the HPI.

O Onset
P Palliative/ Provocative Factors
Q Quality
R Region/Radiation
S Severity
T Timing

Pertinent Positives and Negatives/Associated Symptoms

These are symptoms and facts that pertain to the chief complaint. In the beginning of your training, these are the most challenging to determine, but as your medical knowledge expands, it gets easier. The *Data Gathering* chapter and "column method" later described in this book will facilitate this part of the history.

Ex. *Patient has fever, nausea and vomiting. Denies diarrhea, dysuria, vaginal discharge or having previous abdominal surgery*

By the time you complete your HPI, you should have a clear and concise picture of what is going on.

Ex. *Mary is a 25 year old G1P1 Hispanic female complaining of abdominal pain. The pain began this morning in the right lower abdomen and has lasted 4 hours. She describes the pain as 5/10, pressure feeling, radiating to her pelvis, acetaminophen has not helped, bumps during the car ride make it worse. Patient has fever, nausea and vomiting. Denies diarrhea, dysuria, vaginal discharge or having previous abdominal surgery*

Past Medical History (PMH)

Also called "Problem List", these are the medical problems the patient has currently or has had in the past.

List each diagnosis in order of importance, the dates of diagnosis if possible, and a comment if explanation is necessary.

If the patient states, "I don't have any medical issues," reconfirm by asking about diabetes, hypertension, heart issues, stroke, thyroid disease, cancer, or any other medical conditions that may be the cause of the current symptoms.

Document vaccine status, and we can include Last Menstrual Period (if not included in the HPI)

Ex. *Hypothyroid – 2013, with thyroid nodules*

Preeclampsia – 2014

Breast Lump – 2010 – removed and biopsied, result benign

Family History

This is where you list family members and their medical conditions.

Begin with the parents, then siblings, then grandparents, then distant family if pertinent.

If family member has deceased, document the cause and the age of death.

If the patient thinks the family member has a medical condition but it has not been officially diagnosed, use quotations.

Mother
    Deceased in1998 at age 40 from injuries in a motor vehicle collision

Father
    Alive diabetes

Sister
> *"Bipolar"*

Maternal aunt
> *Breast cancer, in remission*

Past Surgical History (PSH)

Here we list the surgeries, dates and any complications.

If listing hysterectomy, specify the following:

Partial Hysterectomy– cervix remains

Total Hysterectomy – full uterus removed

BSO – bilateral salpingo-oophorectomy – both ovaries removed

SHO – still has ovaries

Ex.
> *C-section - 2014*
> *Right Breast lump removal – 2010*
> *Thyroid biopsy - 2009*

Social History (SH)

Allows you to get to know the patient and possible contributing factors to the illness. These include:

Smoking status – list what they smoke, how many packs a day and how many years

Calculate *Pack Years* by multiplying the number of packs per day smoked X # of years the patient has been smoking

Ex. One who smokes 2 packs a day for 10 years would have a 20 pack year history.

Do they vape? How many cartridges a day?

Drinking status – type of alcohol, how much
Use of recreational drugs
Type of work
Relationship status
Living arrangements
Do they feel safe in their relationship
Sexual history – may have own section
      Ask about partners, monogamous?
      If had unprotected sex?
      If ever had been assaulted or abused
      Any history of STI's (Sexually Transmitted Illnesses)
            Name the date, diagnosis, treatment and if checked for cure

Medications

List the medications and include:

Name - generic or brand name

Route – How is the patient taking the medication

      Oral – po
      Intramuscular – IM
      Intravenously – IV
      Rectally – pr
      Transvaginally - pv
      Sublingual – SL
      Subcutaneous - SC or SubQ

Dose – amount of medication taken in units (most commonly, milligrams)

Frequency – how often are they taking the medication

      Daily – QD

Twice a day – BID
Three times a day – TID
Four times a day – QID
Every other day – QoD
As needed - prn

Compliance – are they taking the medication as directed. If not write "Non-compliant"

Example.

Synthroid 125 mcg one po QD
Orthrotricyclin OCP – forgets to take regularly
acetaminophen - prn

Allergies

List the medications first in order of most severe allergy.

Next list the medications and what happens to the patient when they take the drug.

Then list any other pertinent allergies (IV contrast, food, etc).

If no drug allergies, write NKDA (No Known Drug Allergies).

Example: *Allergies – Penicillin (anaphylaxis), Bactrim (rash). Shrimp (some lip tingling)*

Review of Systems (ROS)

This is when we review the various body systems. We ask using lists of symptoms/conditions per body system.

List the positives of each first and then the negatives. When typing, use italics, underline or bold for positives.

General

Head and Neck

Hematology/Lymphatic

Cardiac

Pulmonary

Gastrointestinal

Genitourinary

Musculoskeletal

Neurological

Psychiatric

Endocrinology

Skin

Dental

Example:

General
feeling tired, chills, body aches, no changes in weight

Head and Neck
denies sore throat or headache

Hematologic/Lymphatic System
no swollen lymph nodes

Cardiac
denies chest pain, palpitations

Pulmonary
denies shortness of breath, cough, hemoptysis

Gastrointestinal
denies loss of appetite, gas, bloating

Genitourinary
denies hematuria, incontinence, abnormal vaginal bleeding

Musculoskeletal
has some low back pain and right hip pain

Neurological
denies dizziness, numbness

Psychiatric
denies depression and anxiety

Endocrinology
denies excessive thirst, intolerance to heat or cold

Skin
denies rashes, pustules

Dental
no pain with chewing, gum tenderness

This concludes the subjective portion, or history. Now we need to examine the patient and obtain objective findings.

Physical Exam

This is what the medical provider finds and reports in a head-to-toe fashion.

List the positives and pertinent negatives for the following:

Vital signs
    Temperature
    Pulse
    Respiratory Rate
    Blood Pressure
    Pulse Oximetry

Height and Weight

General
Head and Neck
Hematology/Lymphatic
Cardiac
Pulmonary
Gastrointestinal
Genitourinary
Pelvic
Musculoskeletal
Neurological
Psychiatric
Endocrinology
Skin
Dental

Example:

Vital signs: Temperature 102.4 degrees F, HR – 112, RR 20, BP 120/76
General
   in moderate distress, slightly pale
Head and Neck
   goiter (enlarged thyroid)
Heme/Lymph
   no purpura, no inguinal lymphadenopathy
Cardiac
   elevated heart rate, no M/R/G (murmurs, rubs or gallops)
Pulmonary
   CTA-B, clear to auscultation bilaterally
Gastrointestinal
   acute tenderness at McBurney's point, guarding, no rebound tenderness,
   positive bowel sounds
Pelvic Exam
   no cervical motion tenderness, pain in the right adnexa, no vaginal
discharge
Musculoskeletal
   mild spasms in the quadratus lumborum, no CVA tenderness, no leg length
   discrepancy

Skin

no rashes or lesions

Assessment

Here is where we list what the patient has based on subjective and objective findings, forming an assessment. We can also include what we think they have by listing our differentials.

Assessment is what they truly have (not a guess)
Differential is what we believe they have (a guess)

For example, if a person comes in with chest pain and you want to rule out heart attack, pneumonia or costochondritis, the chest pain would be the "assessment" as it's undeniable and what they truly have. The "heart attack" or "pneumonia" or "costochondritis" is a guess and not yet confirmed, so that would be included in the differential.

Hence, if lab tests have not yet confirmed your diagnosis, only put what they truly have based on your current assessment.

For example if a female patient presents with fatigue and you want to rule out hypothyroidism, you can only officially assess her to have hypothyroidism if the labs come back confirming it. If not, she is still assessed to have "fatigue" which forces you rule out other differentials.

Then list in order of acuity and importance.

For example if someone presents with chest pain, an ingrown toe nail, and blood in the sputum (hemoptysis), the "ingrown toe nail" would be listed after the "chest pain" and "blood in the sputum (hemoptysis)."

With your differential you can use "rule out (r/o)" or the terms "probable" or "possible."

If greater than 50% sure – use the term probable.

If less than 50% sure – use the term possible.

Example

1. *Right Lower Quadrant (RLQ) Abdominal Pain – probable appendicitis*

2. *Right Pelvic Pain – most likely from #1 but will also r/o pregnancy, ovarian pathology, colitis, UTI, kidney stones, sacroiliitis*

3. *Hypothyroid with nodules*

The Plan

Here we document how we are going to confirm or rule out our differentials/assessments. So we give our plan for what we want our patient to do/have.

These include, but are not limited to:

- Tests (labs, radiology)
- Medications to be prescribed
- Modalities to be used
- Referrals
- Work Restrictions
- Home instructions
- Follow up

Example

1. *Labs: -CBC, Comp, UA, Urine culture, Serum Pregnancy test, vaginal cultures*
2. *If serum pregnancy negative- CT Abdomen and Pelvis*
3. *Pelvic ultrasound (and transvaginal ultrasound)*
4. *If CT Abdomen positive- call surgeon ASAP*
5. *IV fluids, Morphine for pain control*
6. *NPO (no feeding)*
7. *Admit for observation*

Putting it all together - Example

Chief Complaint

Patient presents today saying "I have a tummy ache"

History of Present Illness

Mary is a 25 year old G1P1 Hispanic female complaining of abdominal pain. The pain began this morning in the right lower abdomen and has lasted 4 hours. She describes the pain as 5/10, pressure feeling, radiating to her pelvis, acetaminophen has not helped, bumps during the car ride make it worse. Patient has fever, nausea and vomiting. Denies diarrhea, dysuria, vaginal discharge or having previous abdominal surgery

Allergies

Penicillin (anaphylaxis)
Bactrim (rash)
Shrimp (some lip tingling)

Medications

Synthroid 125 mcg one PO QD
Orthrotricyclin OCP – forgets to take regularly
acetaminophen - prn

Past Medical History

Hypothyroid – 2013, with thyroid nodules
Preeclampsia – 2014
Breast Lump – 2010 – removed and biopsied, result benign

Past Surgical History

C-section - 2014
Right Breast lump removal – 2010
Thyroid biopsy – 2009

Review of Systems

General – feeling tired, chills, body aches, no changes in weight
Head and Neck – denies sore throat or headache
Hematologic/Lymph node – no swollen lymph nodes
Cardiac – denies chest pain, palpitations
Pulmonary – denies shortness of breath, cough, hemoptysis
Gastrointestinal – denies loss of appetite, gas, bloating
Genitourinary – denies hematuria, incontinence, abnormal vaginal bleeding
Musculoskeletal – has some low back pain and right hip pain
Neurological – denies dizziness, numbness
Psychiatric – denies depression and anxiety
Endocrinology – denies excessive thirst, intolerance to heat or cold
Skin – denies rashes, pustules
Dental – no pain with chewing, gum tenderness

Physical Exam

Vitals: Temperature 102.4 degrees F, HR – 112, RR 20, BP 120/76

General – in moderate distress, slightly pale
Head and Neck – goiter (enlarged thyroid)
Heme/Lymph – no purpura, no inguinal lymphadenopathy
Cardiac – elevated heart rate, no M/R/G (murmurs, rubs or gallops)
Pulmonary – CTA-B, clear to auscultation bilaterally
Gastrointestinal – acute tenderness at McBurney's point, guarding, no rebound tenderness, positive bowel sounds
Pelvic Exam – no cervical motion tenderness, pain in the right adnexa, no vaginal discharge
Musculoskeletal – mild spasms in the quadratus lumborum, no CVA tenderness, no leg length discrepancy
Skin – no rashes or lesions

Assessment

1. *Right Lower Quadrant (RLQ) Abdominal Pain – probable appendicitis*
2. *Right Pelvic Pain – most likely from #1 but will also r/o pregnancy, ovarian pathology, colitis, UTI, kidney stones, sacroiliitis*
3. *Hypothyroid with nodules*

Plan

1. *Labs: CBC, Comp, UA, Urine culture, Serum Pregnancy test, Vaginal cultures*
2. *If serum pregnancy negative, CT Abdomen and Pelvis*
3. *Pelvic ultrasound (with transvaginal ultrasound)*
4. *If CT Abdomen positive – call surgeon ASAP*
5. *IV fluids, Morphine for pain control*
6. *NPO (no feeding)*
7. *Admit for observation*

The 15 Minute History and Physical for OSCE

Depending on the rotation we will have anywhere from 10 minutes to an hour to take one's history and physical. But for one's OSCE's, the H&P needs to be done very succinctly. Here's a breakdown of how we have been able to accomplish this.

:00 - :45 Review the *Chief Complaint*, look at the vitals, gather one's thoughts, jot down one's template

:45- 1:30 Enter the room, greet the patient with introductions, use hand sanitizer, sit down

1:30 - 4:00 Obtain the *Chief Complaint, History of Present Illness (OPQRST), Associated Symptoms*

4:00-6:30 Complete the rest of history including *PMH, FH, PSH, Allergies, Meds, SH* and brief *ROS*

6:30 - 11:30 Complete physical, perform OMM (DO students), can ask some additional ROS as you examine or treat the body part

11:30-12:30 - Summarize the findings to the patient and give your *Assessment and Plan*

12:30-13:00 - Offer intervention or assistance with issues such as smoking cessation, diabetes, counseling

13:00-14:00 - Elicit questions and close, leaving after thanking the patient and shaking their hand

Most testing scenarios are 14 minutes, hospital and clinic settings could be shorter or longer. In non-testing settings take the time you need to get a thorough history and exam.

Chapter 8   Tips to Improve Overall Humanism/Bedside Manner

Even though humanism and bedside manner can't be memorized, it can be developed over time with practice.

The following will help demonstrate your professionalism, empathy, communication and interpersonal skills.

1. Dress professionally (clean white coat, business attire, hair pulled back)
2. Knock on the door and smile when you enter
3. Thank the patient for waiting (avoid saying "sorry for your wait" - keep it positive)
4. Greet with a handshake; double-handed may be more sincere but not mandatory
5. Introduce yourself as Student Doctor _____
6. Ask how the patient would like to be addressed
7. Excuse yourself to wash your hands
8. Ask permission to sit, and sit below eye level of the patient
9. Make eye contact
10. Listen to the patient actively, with occasional nods and "I understand."
11. If the patient is in pain ask if there is anything you can do to make them more comfortable
12. If the patient cries, offer a tissue
13. If the patient is distressed, sad, scared, give a reassuring hand on their shoulder
14. Transition smoothly to the physical; let the patient know what you will be examining and why before you touch them
15. Don't use the word "quick" but "brief" instead
16. Offer the drape early and set across their lap so they can use during the exam
17. Listen with the stethoscope on skin and not over clothing. Ask patient to lower the gown to allow access to the heart sounds.

18. Tell the patient what you wish to do and obtain verbal consent. "I would now like to perform an exam, may I listen to your lungs......"

19. Help the patient re-gown and/or drape after exam

20. Offer to help the patient lie back, and pull out the foot rest for them

21. Periodically ask if they are comfortable

22. While the patient is supine ask if they would like to bend their knees to relax the back and abdominal muscles

23. After the exam, roughly around the 2 minute warning, briefly summarize what they came in with and transition to your assessment

24. Let the patient know what you think is going on and what you would like to do for them

25. Ask if they have any questions

26. Shake their hand before leaving and thank them

27. Avoid talking over the patient. If you accidentally interrupt them, apologize and then allow them to speak

28. Remember to always ask "why?" When a patient states they came in for a physical or thinks they have cancer ask "why" because they may reveal some added back-story or other symptoms they've experienced recently.

29. If asked by the patient "Do you think I have cancer?" They are looking for your response and possibly reassurance. You should then ask the patient "what makes you concerned that you have cancer?"

 A good answer might be….

That's a good question, and understandable why you'd be concerned. Even though we couldn't be definitive before the testing, could you answer me these questions? Are you having any weight loss? No? that's good. How is your appetite? Good? well that's reassuring. So we will screen you for _____ cancer but based on what you told me, I'm thinking less severe issues could be causing your current issues.

Closing

When completing an encounter here's some tips:

- Summarize the visit
- Solicit Questions

- Continue eye contact
- Ensure they received what they wanted to from the visit and time with you.
- Shake their hand
- Offer a means to help them with their enlisted items.
- Example: I'm looking forward to seeing you in two weeks. If you have any difficulty checking your sugar, please call my office and I or a nurse will help you through it."

Avoid:

- Chewing gum in front of the patient
- Clicking your pen when you are nervous
- Sitting back in your seat
- Wearing short skirts/high heels
- Hair falling into face
- Touching your face/hair and not washing hands before touching patient

These tips are easy to incorporate into your regular medical persona. Don't forget to include these when you practice your patient encounters.

Chapter 9 Tips to Improve Data Gathering

Data gathering in the medical field relies on one having a plan before examining the patient. So many of us physicians will go into the room having a differential diagnosis ready to go.

For example if one has chest pain we would be thinking we need to rule out a heart attack, pericarditis, pneumonia, etc.

Where some students struggle, however, is coming up with their differential.

This is where the *column method* helps…..

A Peek into How Doctors Think - An Introduction to "Columns"

Anyone who is on their path to becoming a successful physician will easily pass a test such as the clinical skills assessment taken during schooling. So to pass the examination one needs to think like a physician.

We start by looking at the cause and then breaking down what could be occurring resulting in that cause, or in other words, forming a differential diagnosis. So if someone has chest pain, one may form a differential consisting of heart attack, pericarditis and costochondritis. But other issues may be at play such as pneumonia or esophagitis.

So when we look at a person with chest pain, we consider all the body parts or causes that could be causing the symptoms.

Hence with a patient presenting with chest pain, one would consider a cardiovascular cause, pulmonary cause, gastrointestinal cause, musculoskeletal cause, and even psychiatric cause.

This is the basis of forming one's **columns**. For every chief complaint we form columns either mentally or on paper and then ask associated symptoms (or pertinent positives or negatives) to determine which column we're in. Usually a few "power questions" will help discriminate which column you are in. Once you hit the correct column you will ask further questions along that line.

True there are many more questions we could ask than just the "power questions," but during a time crunch we need to ask very specific ones to determine if we are on the right track. If we receive multiple "no"s along a column, we know to move onto the next column.

Hence if a patient with chest pain denies dizziness and diaphoresis or sternal pain upon palpation but admits to cough, shortness of breath and sputum production, we have just narrowed down the chest pain patient to a pulmonary cause as opposed to assuming it was cardiac in nature. Then we would continue down the pulmonary column, thinking our differential may be a pneumonia/bronchitis/pulmonary embolism, and ask about hemoptysis, fever, chills, etc.

When you hear hooves, you typically think horses. OSCE's tend to use cases that are common and avoid testing you on the "zebras" (e.g. acute intermittent porphyria). We will provide columns for various common patient cases and the power questions to help you focus down your differential.

Now these columns can also assist with the <u>physical exam</u> component of data gathering. If the above patient presenting with chest pain could have a cardiac/pulmonary/GI/musculoskeletal condition, one would examine his heart, lungs, upper abdomen and palpate the sternum and ribs.

For an added bonus, the columns can additionally assist one in <u>forming their differential</u> for the SOAP note. Most institutions and examinations prefer at least 3-4 differentials for the chief complaint. Many students have difficulty coming up with the unlikely bottom two differentials. But using the columns one could pick a cause from each column. Hence the above patient with chest pain who admits to cough and sputum production could have an assessment/differential of:

Chest pain r/o
      Pneumonia
      Bronchitis
      PE
      MI
      GERD
      Costochondritis

If a case involves a not so clear-cut symptom, columns could be used as well.

For example let's take a patient presenting with hair loss. If one complains of hair loss, a variety of differentials could be at play. One column could be an endocrinology source (such as hypothyroidism or diabetes), another could be psychological (such as stress or trichotillomania), a third could be medications (such as chemotherapy agents), and a fourth could include genetics. Narrowing these down with power questions could exclude non-contributing columns.

So whether it's a direct body system or cause, columns help one focus down the differential and allow an easy visual that enables one during a timed test to think quickly and know which questions to ask.

Again these columns are instituted after the History of Present Illness in which a student obtains onset/chronology, palliative/provocative factors, quality of symptoms, radiation, severity and timing (OPQRST).

They will be written down in the SOAP note after the HPI.

Example: Mary is a 25 year old female presenting with acute onset right foot pain. It began 6 hours ago after she went for a job. Ice provides some relief but walking on it worsens the pain. The pain is sharp, constant with a severity of 7/10. **She denies fever, chills, open wounds, swelling, redness, temperature changes, numbness or tingling.**

Since during this step in the history most medical students find it challenging to know "which questions to ask," the columns and power questions simplify this. The book *Data Gathering Prep Guide for the Boards* goes into more detail, but here is a summary of columns and power questions for easy reference.

Chest Pain

Cardiovascular	Pulmonary	Gastrointestinal	Musculoskeletal	Psychological
Chest pain?	Cough?	Acid taste?	Pain w/ palpation?	Sad?
SOB?	Sputum?	Burping?	Reproducible?	Anxious?
Palpitations	Fever?	Abdominal Pain?	Pain with ROM?	Issues with sleeping?
Dizziness?	Chills?	Heartburn?	Muscle spasms?	Cry often?
Diaphoresis?	Wheezing?		History of trauma?	Changes in appetite?
	SOB (already asked in cardio column)			

Abdominal Pain (female)

Gastrointestinal	Gynecological	Urological	Musculoskeletal
Fever?	LMP?	Blood in the urine?	Pain upon palpation?
Chills?	Pelvic pain?	Painful urination?	Reproducibility?
Nausea?	Abnormal bleeding?	Urinary frequency?	Pain with ROM?
Vomiting?	Fever/Chills (asked in the GI column already)?		Muscle spasms?
Diarrhea?	Vaginal discharge?		History of trauma?
Constipation?			

Back Pain

Musculoskeletal	Urological	Gastrointestinal	Neurological	Cardiovascular
Pain upon palpation?	Blood in the urine?	Fever?	Numbness?	Chest pain?
Reproducibility?	Painful urination?	Chills?	Tingling?	SOB?
Pain with ROM?	Urinary frequency?	Nausea?	Weakness?	Palpitations?
Muscle spasms?		Vomiting?	Low Back Pain?	Dizziness?
History of trauma?		Diarrhea?	Leg pain?	Diaphoresis?
		Constipation?		Sweating?
		Abdominal Pain?		
		Jaundice?		

Left Shoulder Pain

Musculoskeletal	Neurological	Cardiac	Pulmonary	Gastrointestinal
Pain upon palpation?	Numbness?	Chest Pain?	SOB (already asked in cardiac column)	Abd. Pain?
Reproducibility?	Tingling?	SOB?	Cough?	Fever?
Pain with ROM?	Weakness?	Palpitations?	Sputum?	Chills?
Muscle spasms?	Neck pain?	Dizziness?	Fever?	Nausea?
History of trauma?		Diaphoresis?	Chills?	Vomiting
		Sweating?	Wheezing?	Diarrhea?
				Constipation?

Right Shoulder Pain

Musculoskeletal	Urological	Gastrointestinal	Neurological	Cardiovascular
Pain upon palpation?	Blood in the urine?	Fever?	Numbness?	Chest pain?
Reproducibility?	Painful urination?	Chills?	Tingling?	SOB?
Pain with ROM?	Urinary frequency?	Nausea?	Weakness?	Palpitations?
Muscle spasms?		Vomiting?	Low Back Pain?	Dizziness?
History of trauma?		Diarrhea?	Leg pain?	Diaphoresis?
		Constipation?		Sweating?
		Abdominal Pain?		
		Jaundice?		

Foot Pain

Musculoskeletal	Neurological	Vascular	Endo/Diabetes	Infectious Disease
Pain with Walking?	Numbness?	Temperature change?	Polydipsia?	Fever?
Reproducible?	Tingling?	Color changes?	Polyuria?	Chills?
Pain with ROM?	Leg Weakness?	Swelling?	Weight loss?	Any sores or wounds?
Muscle spasms?	Back pain?	Pain with activity?	Blurry vision?	Redness?
History of trauma?			Nocturia?	Swelling?

Joint Pain

Musculoskeletal	Rheumatological	Infectious disease	Gout
Pain upon palpation?	Symmetry?	Fever?	Recent alcohol?
Reproducibility?	Other joints involved?	Chills?	Recent high protein?
Pain with ROM?	Redness?	Rash?	Recent shellfish?
Muscle spasms?	Swelling?	Insect or Tick bite?	Recent water pill/diuretic?
History of trauma?	Morning stiffness?		

Headache

Neurological	ENT	MSK	Meningitis/ID	Endo/hormones	Psychological
Numbness?	Fever?	Neck pain?	Neck pain?	With menses?	With stress?
Weakness?	Chills?	Pain with palpation?	Photophobia?	Weight changes?	Anxiety?
Tinging?	Sinus drainage?	Reproducibility?	Fever?	Skin changes?	Feel sad?
Memory loss?	Ear pain?	Pain with ROM?	Chills?	Hot/cold intolerance?	Cry easily?
Garbled speech?	Jaw pain?	Muscle spasms?	Malaise?	Polyuria?	Suicidal ideation?
	Sore throat?	Trauma?	Rash?	Polydipsia?	

Fatigue

Sleep	Endocrin.	Heme	Psych	ID	Cardiac	Pulm	Cancer
Hours?	Weight changes?	Easy Bleeding?	Sad?	Fever?	Chest pain?	SOB?	Weight loss?
Restful?	Hair loss?	Bruising?	Crying?	Chills?	Palpitations?	Cough?	Loss of appetite?
Snore?	Skin changes?	Blood in stool?	Anxious?	Sore throat?	Dizziness?	Sputum?	Lumps?
Apnea?	Nocturia?	Vegan?	Unmotivated?	Swollen glands?	Sweating?	Wheeze?	Bleeding?
Drowsy during day?	Hot/cold intolerance?	Pale?	Suicidal?	Rash?	SOB?		

Dizziness

Neuro	Ear/Vestibular	Cardiac	Pulmonary	Heme	ID	Endo/DM
Numbness?	Room spinning?	Chest pain?	SOB (already asked in cardio)	Easy Bleeding?	Fever?	Before eating?
Tingling?	Tinnitus?	Palpitations?	Cough?	Blood in stool?	Chills?	After eating?
Weakness?	Hearing loss?	Lightheadedness?	Sputum?	Easy bruising?	Sore throat?	Weight changes?
Headache?	Ear pain?	Sweating?	Wheeze?	Vegan?	Rash?	Skin changes?
Memory Loss?	Worsens with head movement?	SOB?		Pale?	Dysuria?	Heat/cold intolerance?
Garbled Speech?	Recently sick?					

Physical Exam Table

The following are suggestions you might want to include and document in your basic physical exam and SOAP note based on your columns:

Vitals *	Temperature	Heart rate	Resp. rate	Blood Pressure	Height & Weight
General	Affect	Any distress	Alert	Oriented	
HEENT	PERRLA	Ears	Nares	Mouth	
Neck	Supple	Lymphaden.	Thyroid		
Cardio	Rate	Rhythm	Murmurs	Rubs	Gallops
Pulmonary	CTA-B	Wheezes	Ronchi	Rales	
GI	Tender	Distended	Bowel sounds	Masses	Murphys/McBurney point tenderness
Urological	CVA tender.				
MSK	Range of motion	Spasms	TART changes (PE)	Tenderness upon palpation	
Neuro	DTR's	Sensation	Strength	Straight Leg Raise (if applicable)	Romberg or others if applicable)
Vascular	Note limb temperature	Note limb color	Edema	Pulses	
Heme	Conjunctiva pale/pink?	Skin pallor?			
Sleep (apnea)	Enlarged tonsils?				

* Note: If BMI or pulse oximetry is given with vitals include them as well.

Chapter 10   Sample Practice Cases/Notes

Chest Pain Practice Case

Chest pain is a very popular complaint in the medical setting, as MI and other cardiac pathology can be deadly and must be ruled out first. But many students make the mistake of always thinking cardiac causes, even after its ruled out. So we suggest also including pulmonary, gastrointestinal and musculoskeletal causes in your differentials.

A 51 year old female presents with central chest pain. Onset was this morning, P: worsens with movement and deep inspiration, Q: pain is dull and achy, radiates to neck and shoulder, is constant, 8/10 in severity.

List 4 body systems that could be involved in this patient's chief complaint (what are your columns)?

_____   _____

_____   _____

List 8 associated symptoms (2 from each body system/column) that should be asked regarding the patient's chief complaint:

_____   _____

_____   _____

_____   _____

_____   _____

In addition to Vitals and General, name at least 4 body systems that should be examined based on the patient's chief complaint:

_____   _____

_____   _____

What will your assessment with differentials look like (4 differentials for your first assessment)?

_____

   r/o

_____   _____

_____   _____

Chest Pain Note Example

CC: Left sided chest pain

HPI: Carol is a 51 year old female presenting with Chest Pain that starting this morning, 6AM, when she woke up. This is the first time she experienced this. Movement makes it worse. The pain is constant, radiates to neck and shoulder and nothing alleviates her symptoms. Describes the pain 8/10 in severity and achy The pain worsens with breathing. The chest pain feels as though someone is sitting on her chest. Patient positive for sweats, anxiety, lightheadedness, nausea, and shortness of breath. Patient denies heartburn, pain on inspiration, fever, vomiting, diarrhea, constipation, coughing or sputum production.

Past Medical History
Has mild anxiety diagnosed last year but denies diabetes, heart disease, hypertension, high cholesterol, and previous hospitalizations

Family History

Dad, died of a heart attack, age 52
Mom, well, diabetes in control

Past Surgical History
none

Medication
Xanax 1 mg po q HS

Allergies
Penicillin (rash)

Social History
35 pack years, smoking tobacco, open to quitting
denies alcohol and illicit drugs
sexually active, uses protection
married, lives with husband, monogamous, works as a cashier

Physical Exam

Vitals: Temperature 98.6, HR 92, RR 18, BP 140/90, Pulse ox 97%, BMI 22

General – pleasant, but slightly anxious, appears in mild distress

Neck: No lymph nodes palpated, thyroid not enlarged, no carotid bruits auscultated bilat.

Heart: RRR no murmur, neg. S3, neg. S4

Lungs: CTA bilat, no rales, no wheeze

Musculo-skeletal: positive for somatic dysfunction at T1 thru T4 bilat. with rhomboid spasm. Good forward flexion, Good ROM to all joints and no swelling noted, not tender on palpation of sternum

Assessment
    1. Chest pain – r/o
      MI
      Arrhythmia
      CHF
      Pneumonia - unlikely
      Somatic Dysfunction
      Costochondritis
2. anxiety

3. family History of MI
4. Tobacco use

Plan
1. EKG, Troponin, Cardiac Enzymes, cardiology workup, lipid panel, stress test
2. Chest Xray
3. counseling for smoking cessation
4. Admit to hospital
5. OMM after discharge (MFR, BLT, Counterstrain, and soft tissue techniques- choose type)

Abdominal Pain Practice Case

A 28 year old female presents with RLQ pain. **O**nset was 2 days ago, **P:** worsens with movement, **Q:** pain is dull and achy, denies **r**adiation, is constant, 5/10 in **s**everity.

List 4 **body systems** that could be involved in this patient's chief complaint (what are your **columns**)?

_____   _____

_____   _____

List 8 **associated symptoms** (2 from each body system/column) that should be asked regarding the patient's chief complaint:

_____   _____

_____   _____

_____   _____

_____   _____

In addition to **Vitals** and **General**, name at least 4 body systems that should be examined based on the patient's chief complaint:

_____   _____

_____   _____

What will your assessment with differentials look like (4 differentials for your first assessment)

_____

r/o

_____   _____

_____   _____

Abdominal Pain Note Example

CC: Left lower abdominal pain

HPI: Lila is a 28 year old female presenting with LLQ pain X 2 days. Her LMP was 6 weeks ago but gets them irregularly. Pain has been constant, achy, 5/10 and nothing she does makes it better. She denies fever, chills, nausea, vomiting, constipation or hematuria. She does have some discomfort when she urinates, some vaginal discharge that doesn't itch and loose stool.   **PMH:** none, last PAP normal but was 7 years ago **FH:** Mother had endometrial cancer at age 32, treated, doing well. No surgeries. No medications. No allergies. **SH:** Denies tobacco, denies alcohol, smokes marijuana occasionally, is sexually active and uses condoms "most of the time", works as a lifeguard.
PE Vitals: Temperature 99.9, HR 90, RR 12, BP 110/70, Pulse ox 98%, BMI 22
General: slightly anxious, mild distress, alert & oriented X 3
HEENT: eyes PERRLA, TM clear, canals clear, nares patent, throat pink. Neck supple, thyroid not enlarged
Heme/Lymph: no bruises, no inguinal lymphadenopathy
Heart: RRR no murmur, neg. S3, neg. S4
Lungs: CTA bilat
Abd – soft, tender in left lower quadrant, non distended, + Bowel Sounds, no masses
Pelvic – slight fullness in left adnexa, white discharge noted and cultured, no CMT tenderness, uterus non tender

Assessment
       1. LLQ pain - r/o
  a. Ectopic pregnancy

b. UTI
c. PID
d. Diverticulitis
e. Ovarian cyst rupture
f. Endometrial Cancer

2. Amenorrhea
3. Pelvic fullness/mass
3. Family History of endometrial cancer
4. Marijuana use
5. Unsafe sex practices

Plan
1. Serum HCG, CBC, CMP, TSH, T4, UA, Urine culture, Vaginal cultures
2. Pelvic Ultrasound (transvaginal)
3. CT abdomen/pelvis (if HCG is negative)
3. counseling for safe sex practices
4. Admit to hospital
5. OMM after discharge (MFR, BLT, Counterstrain, and soft tissue techniques- choose type)

Mid Back Pain Practice Case

A 52 year old male presents with mid back pain. **O**nset was 1 week ago, **P:** anti inflammatories do not help, **Q:** pain is burning, denies **r**adiation, is constant, 6/10 in **s**everity.

List 4 **body systems** that could be involved in this patient's chief complaint (what are your **columns**)?

_____   _____

_____   _____

List 8 **associated symptoms** (2 from each body system/column) that should be asked regarding the patient's chief complaint:

_____   _____

_____   _____

_____   _____

_____   _____

In addition to **Vitals** and **General**, name at least 4 body systems that should be examined based on the patient's chief complaint:

_____   _____

_____   _____

What will your assessment with differentials look like (4 differentials for your first assessment)

_____

r/o

_____   _____

_____   _____

Mid Back Pain Note Example

CC: Right mid back pain

HPI: Frank is a 52 year old male presenting with right mid back pain that starting 1 week ago. He can't tell when it started but was on vacation surfing. He had this pain once before on vacation last year. Ibuprofen OTC has not provided relief. Pain is 6/10 and he can't get comfortable when he tries to sleep. The pain is constant, and has no radiation. He denies trauma, rash, urinary frequency, hematuria, dizziness, but does have some heartburn after eating. PMH: heartburn, dx 1 years ago FH: Father pancreatitis at age 60, alive and well. Denies Surgery, takes Prilosec 20 mg once daily, OTC Ibuprofen (200mg) 2 tablets daily for 1 years. SH - Denies tobacco, Drinks two- three gin and tonics a night denies CAGE questions, Works as a construction worker

PE

Vitals: Temperature 99.9, HR 95, RR 12, BP 115/60, Pulse ox 98%, BMI 40

General – in moderate distress, not appearing comfortable, declines lying down due to back pain

Heart: RRR no murmur, neg. S3, neg. S4

Lungs: CTA bilat

Abd: Slight tender epigastric area, negative Murphy's sign, no CVA tenderness bilaterally, no masses, positive bowel sounds

MSK: spasm appreciated along quadratus lumborum, TART changes T4-L1

Assessment

1. Right Mid Back Pain r/o

      a. Pancreatitis

      b. Ulcer

      c. Esophageal cancer with metz to the back

      d. Cholecystitis

      e.Thoracic strain

2. Heartburn/GERD

3. Alcohol use

4. Obesity

Plan

1. CBC, CMP, Amylase, Lipase, UA, CPK

2. CT abdomen, abdominal ultrasound

3. Pain control (IV in CT positive for pancreatitis)

4. OMM for muscle strain once stable (MFR, BLT, Counterstrain, and soft tissue techniques- choose type)

5. Admit to hospital for testing

6. Counseling on alcohol use/AA

7. Counsel on diet and exercise, once stable

Left Low Back Pain Practice Case

A 63 year old male presents with left low back pain. **O**nset was 6 weeks ago, **P:** Ibuprofen OTC helps occasionally, **Q:** pain is burning, denies **r**adiation, is constant, 4/10 in **s**everity.

List 4 **body systems** that could be involved in this patient's chief complaint (what are your **columns**)?

_____   _____

_____   _____

List 8 **associated symptoms** (2 from each body system/column) that should be asked regarding the patient's chief complaint:

_____   _____

_____   _____

In addition to **Vitals** and **General**, name at least 4 body systems that should be examined based on the patient's chief complaint:

_____   _____

_____   _____

What will your assessment with differentials look like (4 differentials for your first assessment)

_____

r/o

_____   _____

_____   _____

Low Back Pain Note Example

CC: Left low back pain

HPI: Brad is a 63 year old male presenting with left low back pain that starting 6 weeks ago. He can't tell when it started but it's been gradually increasing. Ibuprofen OTC helps occasionally. Pain is 4/10 on most days but after a long day of standing rises to 7/10. Massage used to help but not anymore. The pain is constant, and has no radiation. He denies trauma, rash, abdominal pain, leg pain, numbness or tingling, but does have some issues starting his urine stream and maintaining it. He also finds his urine to be dark and bubbly more than usual but no dysuria or gross blood seen. PMH: HTN, dx 10 years ago FH: Father diabetes DX at age 60, alive at age 90 and well. Denies Surgery, takes Benicar 20 mg once daily for blood pressure, OTC Ibuprofen (200mg) prn SH – smokes cigars rarely, no more often than once a month. Works at the local nuclear reactor as a radiation screener.

PE

Vitals: Temperature 98.6, HR 80, RR 12, BP 150/95, Pulse ox 98%, BMI 30

General – in mild distress, lying on the table on his left side

Heart: RRR no murmur, neg. S3, neg. S4

Lungs: CTA bilat

Abd: NT/ND + BS no masses, rectal exam not performed

MSK: spasm appreciated along left quadratus lumborum, TART changes T4-L1

Assessment

1. Low back pain r/o

    a. Strain/sprain

    b. Pyelonephritis

    c. Urolithiasis

    d. Prostatitis

    e. Metastatic disease

    f. AAA rupture (unlikely)

2. Bubbly urine - r/o proteinuria and diabetes

3. Poor urinary stream - r/o benign prostatic hyperplasia

3. Hypertension

4. Family History of Diabetes

5. Tobacco use

Plan

1. Lumbar spine xray
2. Prostate exam
3. CBC, CMP, PSA, UA, urine microalbumin, urine culture, Hba1C
4. Abdominal ultrasound, consider CT abdomen and pelvis
5. NSAIDs for pain control
6. OMM for muscle strain (MFR, BLT, Counterstrain, and soft tissue techniques-choose type)
7. Recheck BP when not in pain, may need to increase Benicar or add second agent
8. Counseling on smoking cessation
9. Follow up in 1-2 days

Right Knee Pain Practice Case

A 48 year old male presents with right knee pain. **O**nset was 8 am this morning, **P:** Ibuprofen OTC gives no relief, **Q:** pain is burning, denies **r**adiation, is constant, 10/10 in **s**everity.

List 4 **body systems** that could be involved in this patient's chief complaint (what are your **columns**)?

_____   _____

_____   _____

List 8 **associated symptoms** (2 from each body system/column) that should be asked regarding the patient's chief complaint:

_____   _____

_____   _____

In addition to **Vitals** and **General**, name at least 4 body systems that should be examined based on the patient's chief complaint:

_____   _____

_____   _____

What will your assessment with differentials look like (4 differentials for your first assessment)

_____

r/o

_____   _____

_____   _____

Right Knee Pain Note Example

CC: Right knee pain

HPI: Michael is a 48 year old male presenting with right knee pain that starting yesterday morning, 8AM, upon waking up. This is the first time he experienced this. Ibuprofen OTC has not provided relief. Pain is so severe 10/10 he can't put his pants on. The pain is constant, and has no radiation. He states the knee is very swollen and is hot to the touch. He denies trauma, prior injuries to his extremities, fever, chills or redness. He states no other joints are involved. **PMH:** Arthritis in his low back, HTN well controlled, dx 3 years ago

FH
Grandfather stomach cancer, died at age 60
Father – HTN still alive

PSH - none

Medication
HCTZ 25 mg once daily
OTC Ibuprofen (200mg) 4 tablets daily for 2 years

Allergies -NKDA

SH - Denies tobacco
Drinks two- three scotches a night with more on the weekends, denies CAGE questions
Is not sexually active
Works as a Poker dealer
ROS – has intermittent abdominal pain, low back pain, but denies numbness, tingling, hematuria, dysuria or blood in the stool

PE

Vitals: Temperature 98.7, HR 100, RR 14, BP 150/100, Pulse ox 98%, BMI 32

General – in moderate distress, standing, not wanting to sit down, anxious
Neck: Supple, no lymphadenopathy, no carotid bruits

Heart: RRR no murmur, neg. S3, neg. S4
Lungs: CTA bilat
Abd – soft, NT/ND + Bowel Sounds, no masses
MSK: Right knee markedly swollen, slightly erythematous, very limited range of motion,
2+ DP pulses, 2+ PT pulses, 1+ DTRs, no ankle edema, right hip and ankle- no gross
abnormalities
Low back – positive spasms along quadratus lumborum, limited ROM

Assessment

1. Right knee pain – r/o
   Gout
   Septic arthritis
   Osteoarthritis
   Rheumatoid arthritis

2. Low Back Pain
3. Excessive NSAID use
4. abdominal pain – possible secondary to #3
5. moderate alcohol use
6. Family history of stomach cancer
7. HTN
8. Obesity

Plan
1. Knee aspiration, colchicine, CBC, Comp panel, uric acid, ESR, HBA1C, lipid panel
2. Knee Xray
3. Lumbar spine xray
4. Discontinue NSAIDS, consider pain management
5. Alcohol use counseling
6. Refer to GI (abd pain), cardio (HTN), nutrition
7. Consider d/c HCTZ due to possible gout and change to Norvasc 5mg daily
8. OMM Lumbar Spine (MFR, BLT, Counterstrain, and soft tissue techniques- choose type)
9. Follow up 1 week

Sore Throat Practice Case

A 48 year old male presents with sore throat. **O**nset was 1 month ago, **P:** Gargling with salt water helps occasionally, **Q:** pain is burning, denies **r**adiation, is constant, 6/10 in **s**everity.

List 4 **body systems** that could be involved in this patient's chief complaint (what are your **columns**)?

_____   _____

_____   _____

List 8 **associated symptoms** (2 from each body system/column) that should be asked regarding the patient's chief complaint:

_____   _____

_____   _____

_____   _____

_____   _____

In addition to **Vitals** and **General**, name at least 4 body systems that should be examined based on the patient's chief complaint:

_____   _____

_____   _____

What will your assessment with differentials look like (4 differentials for your first assessment)

_____

r/o

_____   _____

_____   _____

Sore Throat Note Example

CC: Sore throat

HPI: Larry is a 48 year old male presenting with sore throat for 1 month. He doesn't recall when it started, except maybe he had spicy food that day. He has decreased energy and pain with swallowing. He's gargled with salt water which helps a little. Severity is 6/10 and feels like a burning. He denies fever, rash, n/v, chills, but does have an acid taste in his mouth and "swelling" in his neck.

PMH: none, denies DM, HTN, heart issues, thyroid issues or history of cancer **FH:** Both parents are alive but have HTN. No surgeries. No medications. No allergies. **SH:** Smokes 1 ppd X 25 years. Is sexually active, but practices "safe sex" as he states he only performs oral sex. He works as a vocal coach. Denies any recent vaccines.

PE Vitals: Temperature 98.6, HR 80, RR 14, BP 120/70, Pulse ox 98%, BMI 31

General: blunted affect, NAD, A&O X 3

HEENT: eyes PERRLA, TM clear, canals clear, nares patent, throat pink. Neck supple, thyroid not enlarged, tonsils 3+/3+

Heme/Lymph: no bruises, 2+ right anterior cervical lymphadenopathy

Heart: RRR no murmur, neg. S3, neg. S4

Lungs: CTA bilat

Abd – soft, NT/ND + Bowel Sounds, no masses

Assessment

1.   Sore throat – r/o

    a.   Strep or viral pharyngitis

    b.   Infectious mononucleosis

    c.   Throat cancer

    d. Vocal strain

    e. GERD

    f. Acute lymphadenitis

2. Energy loss/fatigue

3. Dysphagia

4. Lymphadenopathy

5. Tobacco use

6. Unsafe sex practices

Plan

1. CBC, CMP, Monospot, throat culture, strep screen, TSH, Free T4
2. ENT referral or perform NPL
3. PPI for GERD symptoms
4. Counsel on smoking cessation and safe sex practices
5. Follow up 1 week

Fatigue Practice Case

A 56 year old female presents with fatigue. **O**nset was 2 months ago, **P:** caffeine offers no relief **Q:** fatigue is constant and worsening, 5/10 in **s**everity.

List 4 **body systems** that could be involved in this patient's chief complaint (what are your **columns**)?

_____   _____

_____   _____

List 8 **associated symptoms** (2 from each body system/column) that should be asked regarding the patient's chief complaint:

_____   _____

_____   _____

_____   _____

_____   _____

In addition to **Vitals** and **General**, name at least 4 body systems that should be examined based on the patient's chief complaint:

_____   _____

_____   _____

What will your assessment with differentials look like (4 differentials for your first assessment)

_____

r/o

_____   _____

_____   _____

Fatigue Note Example

CC: Fatigue

HPI: Roberta is a 56 year old female presenting with fatigue X 2 months, despite sleeping 7 hours a night. This is constant and gradually worsening over the last few weeks. Caffeine has not provided relief. Fatigue is rated in severity as 5/10. She falls asleep at work often. Her husband notices she snores but does not have witnessed apnea. She hasn't had a physical in 30 years since her last child. It was complicated

by a post partum hemorrhage so she's afraid to go back to the doctor. Also denies fever, chills, dizziness. She complains when she brushes her teeth her gums bleed.
PMH: Last doctor appointment 30 years ago with complicated post partum hemorrhage.
PSH: Appendectomy age 6 **FH:** Father colon cancer, died age 62, Mother – well still alive. No medications or allergies. **SH** - Denies tobacco and alcohol, has husband but a boyfriend when she travels for work. Works as a flight attendant. **ROS** – bruises easily, intermittent abdominal pain and constipation

PE Vitals: Temperature 98.6, HR 80, RR 12, BP 110/60, Pulse ox 98%, BMI 25

General – NAD, pleasant affect, alert
HEENT – eyes conjunctiva pale, PERRLA, TM clear, nares patent, throat pink, no light sensitivity
Neck: Supple, no lymphadenopathy, no carotid bruits
Heart: RRR no murmur, neg. S3, neg. S4
Lungs: CTA bilat
Abd – soft, NT/ND + Bowel Sounds, no masses
MSK: not tested

Assessment
1. Fatigue r/o –
   a. Iron deficient anemia
   b. sleep apnea
   c. depression
   d. colon cancer
   e. hypothyroidism
2. Sleep apnea
3. History of post partum hemorrhage
4. Gum bleeding - r/o periodontitis
5. Family history of colon cancer
6. Non monogamous relationship
7. Abdominal pain
8. Constipation

Plan
1. CBC, CMP, UA, serum HCG, TSH, free T4, stool occult blood, PT, PTT
2. Colonoscopy
3. Seep Study
4. Counseling
5. Follow up 1-2 days

Headache Practice Case

A 52 year old male presents with headache. **O**nset was this morning, **P:** Ibuprofen OTC offers no relief, **Q:** pain is throbbing, denies **r**adiation, is constant, 10/10 in **s**everity.

List 4 **body systems** that could be involved in this patient's chief complaint (what are your **columns**)?

_____   _____

_____   _____

List 8 **associated symptoms** (2 from each body system/column) that should be asked regarding the patient's chief complaint:

_____   _____

_____   _____

In addition to **Vitals** and **General**, name at least 4 body systems that should be examined based on the patient's chief complaint:

_____   _____

_____   _____

What will your assessment with differentials look like (4 differentials for your first assessment)

_____

r/o

_____   _____

_____   _____

Headache Note Example

CC: Headache

HPI: Robert is a 52 year old male presenting with acute headache that started this morning, 6AM, waking him up from sleep. This is the first time he experienced this. Ibuprofen and acetaminophen OTC has not provided relief. Pain is so severe 9/10 he barely could get into the car to come to clinic. The pain is throbbing, and has no radiation. He noticed some pimples near his left eye but gets occasional acne. He feels dizzy and a little drunk even though he doesn't drink alcohol. He denies trauma, prior head injury and neck pain. Also denies fever, chills, visual changes. **PMH:** Cervical disc herniation from car accident 12 years ago, HTN not controlled, has not seen a PCP in years or started medication. **FH:** Father hemorrhagic stroke, died at age 61, Mother still alive but has HTN. No surgeries. For medications takes prn Ibuprofen and acetaminophen OTC. Is allergic to sulfa, saying it causes a rash. **SH** - Denies tobacco and alcohol, is monogamous with his wife, works as an air traffic controller, **ROS** – not obtained

PE Vitals: Temperature 98.6, HR 115, RR 14, BP 180/110, Pulse ox 98%, BMI 30
General – in acute distress, holding his head in his hands
HEENT – eyes PERRLA, TM clear, nares patent, throat pink, no light sensitivity
Neck: Supple, no lymphadenopathy, no carotid bruits
Heart: RRR no murmur, neg. S3, neg. S4
Lungs: CTA bilat
Abd – Soft, NT/ND + Bowel Sounds, no masses
MSK: Trapezium spasm noted bilaterally, neck, limited ROM due to pain.

Assessment
1. Headache r/o –
   a. Meningitis
   b. Shingles
   c. CVA (ischemic or hemorrhagic)
   d. cervicogenic headache

2. History of cervical disc disease
3. HTN - not controlled
4. Somatic dysfunction
5. Family history of hemorrhagic stroke

Plan
1. CBC, CMP, UA, Lumbar Puncture, Varicella IgM
2. CT head without contrast, and if negative, with contrast
3. OMM if stable
4. Metoprolol 25 mg or Lisinopril 10 mg and titrate up
5. OMM if stable (MFR, BLT, Counterstrain, and soft tissue techniques- choose type)
6. Admit to hospital

Low Energy/Fatigue Practice Case

A 26 year old female presents with low energy. **O**nset was 4 months ago, **P:** caffeine offers no relief, **T:** waxes and wanes and is worsening, 9/10 in **s**everity.

List 4 **body systems** that could be involved in this patient's chief complaint (what are your **columns**)?

_____   _____

_____   _____

List 8 **associated symptoms** (2 from each body system/column) that should be asked regarding the patient's chief complaint:

_____   _____

_____   _____

In addition to **Vitals** and **General**, name at least 4 body systems that should be examined based on the patient's chief complaint:

_____   _____

_____   _____

What will your assessment with differentials look like (4 differentials for your first assessment)

_____

r/o

_____   _____

_____   _____

Low Energy/Fatigue Note Example

CC: Low energy, fatigue

HPI: Julia is a 26 year old female presenting with fatigue X 4 months, despite sleeping 8 hours a night. This is gradually worsening over the last few weeks and comes and goes throughout the day. Caffeine has not provided relief. Fatigue is rated in severity as 9/10. She falls asleep in class. Her husband denies snoring or witnessed apnea, but says she looks mad all the time and they have been fighting more often. Her last PE was 1 year ago and her Pap was normal. No blood work done. She denies brusing, easy bleeding, fever, chills, dizziness, or depression. She complain of slight SOB and she's been sweating more and is wondering if she's having hot flashes. LMP 2 weeks ago and was normal. **PMH:** hyperhidrosis diagnosed by dermatologist, anxiety by school couselor.
PSH: Appendectomy age 16 **FH:** Adopted No medications or allergies. **SH** - Denies tobacco and alcohol, has husband but poor sex life lately. Is a medical student.
PE Vitals: Temperature 98.6, HR 100, RR 12, BP 110/60, Pulse ox 98%, BMI 17
General – anxious appearing, pacing in room
HEENT – eyes conjunctiva pink, prominent whites of the eyes, PERRLA, TM clear, nares patent, throat pink, no light sensitivity, thyroid slightly enlarged
Neck: Supple, no lymphadenopathy, no carotid bruits
Heart: tachycardic, and irregular rhythm , neg. S3, neg. S4
Lungs: CTA bilat
Abd – soft, NT/ND + Bowel Sounds, no masses
MSK: not tested

Assessment

2. Fatigue r/o –
      b. Hyperthryoid
      b. Hypothyroid
      c. Anxiety/depression
      d. Sleep apnea
      e. Narcolepsy
      f. Anemia (unlikely)
      g. Pregnancy
2. Shortness of Breath
3. Hyperhidrosis
4. Thyromegaly
5. Tachycardia
6. Relationship issues

Plan

1. CBC, CMP, UA, serum HCG, TSH, free T4, stool occult blood, PT, PTT
2. EKG
3. CXR
4. Thyroid ultrasound
5. Counseling
5. Follow up 1-2 days

Right Foot Pain

A 45 year old female presents with right foot pain. **O**nset was 2 weeks ago, **P:** Ibuprofen OTC helps occasionally, **Q:** pain is burning, denies **r**adiation, is constant, 4/10 in **s**everity.

List 4 **body systems** that could be involved in this patient's chief complaint (what are your **columns**)?

_____   _____

_____   _____

List 8 **associated symptoms** (2 from each body system/column) that should be asked regarding the patient's chief complaint:

_____   _____

_____   _____

In addition to **Vitals** and **General**, name at least 4 body systems that should be examined based on the patient's chief complaint:

_____   _____

_____   _____

What will your assessment with differentials look like (4 differentials for your first assessment)

_____

r/o

_____   _____

_____   _____

Right Foot Pain Note Example

CC: Right foot pain

HPI: Marisol is a 45 year old female presenting with right foot pain that started 2 weeks ago. She doesn't recall any particular trauma but it happened after her 45th birthday party when they went to a club. Ibuprofen OTC provides minimal relief. Pain is burning and sometimes wakes her up at night 8/10. Currently its 4/10.   The pain is intermittent, and has no radiation. She denies recent trauma, but has twisted her foot with her prior coaching job. Denies fever, chills or redness. She does get tingling, and at times her foot feels cold. PMH: Low Vitamin D and recently diagnosed with osteoporosis. Denies DM but sugar was 'borderline high' 6 months ago. LMP 2 weeks ago FH: Both parents are alive but have Type II Diabetes. No surgeries. Medications none regularly except the prn Ibuprofen. No allergies. SH: Denies tobacco, Drinks two- three glasses of wine a night and likes to hit the clubs every weekend, denies CAGE questions, Is not sexually active, Works as a softball coach.

PE Vitals: Temperature 98.7, HR 80, RR 14, BP 120/70, Pulse ox 98%, BMI 29

General: in mild distress, guarding her right foot.

Heme/Lymph: no edema bilaterally, Dorsalis pedis pulses and Posterior tibialis pulses 1+

Heart: RRR no murmur, neg. S3, neg. S4

Lungs: CTA bilat

Abd – soft, NT/ND + Bowel Sounds, no masses

MSK: Right foot demonstrates mild bunion. Good ROM of ankle. No lesions, or ulcer

Neuro: decreased sensation on pinwheel test bilaterally

Assessment

1.   Right foot pain – r/o

    a.   Neuropathy (diabetic or lumbar)

    b.   Peripheral Vascular Disease

    c.   Stress fracture

    d.   Sprain/strain

    e.   Osteomyelitis

    f.   Gout

    g.   plantar fasciitis

2. Borderline DM

3. Vitamin D Deficiency

4. Family History of DM

5. Moderate alcohol use/abuse

Plan

1. CBC, CMP, UA, HbA1C, serum HCG, serum uric acid, vitamin D, Lipid panel
2. Right foot xray
3. ABIs
4. Arterial and venous ultrasound of right lower extremity
5. OMM right foot (MFR, BLT, Counterstrain, and soft tissue techniques- choose type)
6. Alcohol use counseling, AA

7. Follow up 1 week

Dizziness Practice Case

A 72 year old male presents with dizziness. **O**nset was 1 week ago, **P:** He tried Benadryl/diphenhydramine with no success to alleviate symptoms, T: multiple times a day at a severity of 7/10

List 4 **body systems** that could be involved in this patient's chief complaint (what are your **columns**)?

_____   _____

_____   _____

List 8 **associated symptoms** (2 from each body system/column) that should be asked regarding the patient's chief complaint:

_____   _____

_____   _____

In addition to **Vitals** and **General**, name at least 4 body systems that should be examined based on the patient's chief complaint:

_____   _____

_____   _____

What will your assessment with differentials look like (4 differentials for your first assessment)

_____

r/o

Dizziness Note Example

CC: Dizzy

HPI: Thomas is a 72 year old male presenting with dizziness for one week. It began after last week's BBQ in which there was a lot of kids running around and splashing in the pool. He felt fine and swam that day but symptoms began a couple days later as he describes as "room spinning" multiple times a day at a severity of 7/10. He denies ear pain, but states left side feels "plugged." He tried Benadryl/diphenhydramine with no success to alleviate symptoms. He denies chest pain, palpitations, shortness of breath, easy bleeding, easy bruising, headache, garbled speech, numbness or tingling in his extremities, or feelings of dizziness before or after eating.

PMH: ablation for atrial fibrillation
FH: Mother died of a CVA ag 75, Father unknown

Medications: Benadryl for prn allergies

Allergies: none

SH: Retired, denies tobacco use, drug use or alcohol use.

PE
Vitals: Temperature 98.6, HR 60, RR 12, BP 120/70, Pulse ox 98%, BMI 28
General – normal appearing female, NAD, A & O X 3, normal affect
HEENT - left ear canal clear of wax, tympanic membrane retracted, slightly injected, right tympanic membrane unremarkable
Left TMJ mild crepitus
Neck – supple, no LN, trachea midline, thyroid not enlarged
Heart: RRR no murmur, neg. S3, neg. S4
Lungs: CTA bilat
Abd: NT/ND + BS no masses
Pelvic: No gross abnormalities
MSK: slight spasm noted along the left sternocleidomastioid

Assessment

1. Dizziness r/o
    a. Otitis Media
    b. Labrynthitis
    c. BPPV
    d. CVA
    e. Anemia
    f. Atrial fibrillation
    g. Diabetes

2. Allergic rhinitis
3. History of atrial fibrillation
4. Family History of CVA
5. TMJ arthralgia
6. Cervical somatic dysfunction

Plan

1. CT Head with and without contrast, or MRI brain
2. Hallpike maneuver
3. CBC, CMP, TSH, free T4, HbA1C
4. Dental Consult
5. Amoxicillin 500 mg TID X 10 days
6. OMM cervical region (MFR, BLT, Counterstrain, and soft tissue techniques-choose type)
7. Admit to hospital for tests, or if CT negative follow up in 1 week

Amenorrhea Sample Case

CC: No periods

HPI: Brenda is a G0P0 19 year old female presenting with amenorrhea for 3 months. Last year her periods began getting lighter until she only received a few spots. Now no bleeding for 3 months. Feels low energy and pelvic cramps at time but denies discharge or bleeding. She denies trauma, assault, fever, chills, rash, constipation, weight gain and denies increased appetite. In fact she only eats 500 calories a day. She is training for the Olympics in competitive swimming. **PMH:** none except for a broken femur 2 years ago. **FH:** Father depression but stable, Mom has hyperthyroidism. Denies

Surgery, takes no medications. **SH** – denies tobacco, no alcohol, no marijuana. Single, sexually active but uses condoms occasionally. Works as a lifeguard.

PE

Vitals: Temperature 98.6, HR 80, RR 12, BP 110/60, Pulse ox 98%, BMI 15

General – Thin appearing female, NAD, A & O X 3, flat affect

Neck – supple, no LN, trachea midline, thyroid not enlarged

Heart: RRR no murmur, neg. S3, neg. S4

Lungs: CTA bilat

Abd: NT/ND + BS no masses

Pelvic: No gross abnormalities

MSK: TART changes along L1-L4

Assessment

1. Amenorrhea r/o
   a. Pregnancy
   b. Female Athlete Triad
   c. Hyper/hypothryoid
   d. PCOS

2. History of broken femur - rule out osteoporosis, hyperparathyroidism
3. Unsafe sex practices
4. Lumbar somatic dysfunction
5. Low calorie intake

Plan

1. Serum Pregnancy, CBC, CMP, TSH, Free T4, LH, FSH, Vitamin D
2. DEXA scan, Pelvic ultrasound (with trans vaginal)
3. Counsel on safe sex practices
4. OMM Lumbar region
5. Nutrition counselling
6. Follow up in 1-2 weeks

Depression Sample Case

CC: Possible depression

HPI: Lupe is a 48 year old female presenting feeling in a funk for 3 months. She doesn't recall any particular event that triggered it but feels "poor". Has decreased energy and has gained 20 lbs recently. She's been eating more carbs to get some "pleasure in her life" but thinks the weight gain is more than it should. Her LMP was 3 months ago. If she had to rate the severity of her low mood, she would rate it as not horribly low but "getting there". Denies cold intolerance, abnormal menstrual bleeding, poor sleep, suicidal or homicidal ideation. She does however, notice loss of hair and her skin feels dry. She states she has poor diet and fluid intake. **PMH:** none, hasn't had a PE in years. **FH:** Both parents are alive but have HTN. No surgeries. No medications. No allergies. **SH**: Denies tobacco, denies alcohol, smokes marijuana daily since her roommates do, Is not sexually active, works as a bank teller.

PE Vitals: Temperature 98.6, HR 80, RR 14, BP 120/70, Pulse ox 98%, BMI 31
General: blunted affect, NAD, A&O X 3
HEENT: eyes PERRLA, TM clear, canals clear, nares patent, throat pink. Neck supple, thyroid not enlarged
Heme/Lymph: no bruises, no lymphadenopathy supraclavicular
Heart: RRR no murmur, neg. S3, neg. S4
Lungs: CTA bilat
Abd – soft, NT/ND + Bowel Sounds, no masses

Assessment

1. Depression – r/o
    a. Hypothyroidism
    b. Poor nutrition
    c. Marijuana induced depression
    d. PCOS
    e. Menopause
2. Amenorrhea - r/o pregnancy, PCOS
3. Weight Gain
4. Hair loss
5. Dry skin
6. Poor diet
7. Family History of HTN

Plan

1. Serum HCG, FSH, LH, estradiol, progesterone, TSH, free T4
2. Counsel on marijuana use
3. Nutrition consult

4. Behavioral or Cognitive therapy
5. Follow up 1 week

Erectile Dysfunction Sample Case

CC: Things don't work

HPI: Michael is a 48 year old male presenting with erectile dysfunction that has gradually worsened over the last year. His brother's Viagra helps. He denies trauma to the genitals, stress, prior injuries to his extremities, fever, chills, difficulty urinating, or stooling. He has occasional chest pain which his twin brother states is GERD since he has the same. PMH: no doctor visit in years FH: Grandfather diabetes died of old age 92, Father has stable diabetes, doing well. No surgeries. Medications none regular except for prn Viagra. No allergies. SH: Smokes 1 ppd X 30 years. Is not sexually active since he is single and embarrassed., Works as a bartender.

PE Vitals: Temperature 98.7, HR 100, RR 14, BP 150/100, Pulse ox 98%, BMI 32

General – NAD, flat affect.

Neck: Supple, no lymphadenopathy, no carotid bruits

Heart: RRR no murmur, neg. S3, neg. S4

Lungs: CTA bilat

Abd – soft, NT/ND + Bowel Sounds, no masses

MSK: no acute changes, no spasm, no SD noted

Neuro: not done

GU – prostate smooth, symmetrical no masses, elastic, soft

Testes – both descended, no masses, non tender

Penis – circumcised, no lesions

Assessment

1. Erectile Dysfunction – r/o

      a. Arteriosclerosis

      b. Low Testosterone

      c. psychogenic causes

      d. hypothyroid

      e. neurogenic cause

2. History of chest pain

3. Family history of GERD

4. Family history of diabetes

5. Tobacco use

Plan

1. CBC, CMP, HBA1C, TSH, T4, free and total testosterone, UA, Cardiac enzymes, Troponin

2. EKG, Chest xray, stress test

3. Counseling on tobacco use

4. Trial of PDE5 inhibitor

5. Follow up in 1-2 days after testing

Chapter 11 Preparing for Your Standardized Patient Encounters

This next chapter addresses specifically what you will do in a standardized patient encounter and not in real life patient settings.

Be there early before the OSCE or test starts

If travelling, plan on coming into town at least 24 hours in advance in case there is a plane delay and to ensure adequate sleep. Eat a good breakfast the day of the test and arrive at least 30 minutes early.

Always Remember to Bring:

- Professional dress (and extra on hand)
- Clean white coat
- Stethoscope
- Pens

How to Prepare Ahead of Time for Standardized Patient Encounters/OSCE's:

- Find one partner and do practice cases in an OSCE lab on school campus.
- Practice every case as if it were the real exam.
- For every case, one person is the doctor and one is the patient. The patient (robot) has the book in hand as they are being interviewed by the doctor.
- Both students type a timed note at the end of the encounter, and the patient gives the doctor feedback when they finish the note.
- Cross reference the review texts for ways to improve the encounter and the note.
- Each case should take just under 30 mins to perform and review.
- Organize a mini-clinical skills assessment among classmates. Some students with successful pass rates put together a day where multiple cases were performed back-to-back with each student taking the role of physician and then

SP as another student took on the role as physician. This gave not only practice for a clinical skills assessment but also allowed each student to see the perspective of the "SP", improving their scores and pass rate.

During the Encounter - What to do Before Entering the Room

- Student usually receives patient info, chief complaint, and vitals before entering.
- Take 30 seconds to a minute before entering the room.
- Write down template or mnemonics such as CHRPFMASS/OPQRST (explained later).
- Review the information and come up with at least three differentials.
- Always knock!

During the Encounter - What to Do After Entering the Room:

"Mr./Ms. X?"

Get clipboard/paper down on chair or counter

"Hello. My name is student doctor X, pleasure to meet you."

Double hand-shake (may be more warm than a single-handed hand shake, but maintain eye-contact)* + "How would you like to be addressed?"

"Excuse me while I sanitize my hands." + *Hand sanitizer; eyes still on the patient* + "How are you today?"

"Let me get you this drape for some extra privacy."

Unfold drape, place over patient's lap, grab clipboard and sit down

"What brings you in today?"

During the encounter - History, Physical, Assessment and Plan:

CHRPFMASS
- CC
- HPI: **OPQRST**
- ROS
- PMH
- Family
- Medications
- Allergies
- Surgical

- Social

Side notes:

- A student should not ask open-ended questions about the chief complaint.
  - "Are you having any symptoms?"
  - Be specific in your ROS questions to hone in on the right diagnosis.
- On the other hand, open-ended questions are very useful when addressing an emotional concern or conveying humanism.
  - "How did that make you feel?"

- Always sanitize hands before starting a physical exam.
  - If contamination, re-sanitize.
- A student should always let the robot know they are about to begin a physical exam and what they are going to examine/why.
- Problem focused exam + pertinent OMM exam (for osteopathic students only) + heart and lungs.
- Everything the student auscultates, percusses, or palpates should be on bare skin.

Since these are SP encounters and not real-life patient encounters, students will not be allowed to perform the following:
- Adjusting patient's undergarments for any reason.
- Attempting to perform genito-urinary, pelvic, rectal, prostate, breast, or corneal reflex exams (although these can be brought up and typed into the plan section of the SOAP note).
- Auscultation, palpation, inspection through the gown.

Osteopathic Manual Medicine (OMM)

- Rate their pain on a 1-10 scale **before and after** the treatment.
- Students shouldn't perform HVLA. This avoids any injury to the robots. Articulatory techniques should be gentle and without thrusts (rib raising).
- Since OMM takes time to perform, these encounters may take longer.
- Even if the case is a non-OMM encounter, doing a pertinent OMM evaluation on each patient may lead you to an extra differential.

During the Encounter - Before Leaving the Room:

- Give the patient a summary and a plan.
- Always tell the patient to follow up in X amount of time. (if an emergent case admit to the hospital, for all others a 1-2 day or 1 week follow up is safe.
- Always ask if they have any more questions.

- Shake their hand again, smile, tell them "Thank you for coming in."
- Know that once you leave the room, you typically are not allowed to walk back in, even if you have time left over on the encounter.
- Know that any extra time left over after an encounter is typically already added/running on the SOAP note.

After the Encounter - SOAP Notes

- An examinee should **NEVER** place anything into their subjective/objective sections that they did not discuss/perform in the room with the robot.
- Any labs, x-rays, EKGs given outside the room should be reported in the **objective** section of the note.
- The assessment should have **at least 3 differentials** or **3 problem lists/risk factors for disease**.
- Be specific in the plan; "Serum electrolytes, troponins" rather than "blood tests."
- Don't make up your abbreviations, use standardized industry terms

Chapter 12 Timeline of Medical School Milestones

First Year First Semester

Learn the basics of a history and physical, and communication skills in lecture.

Don't worry too much about board exam preparation just yet; this is the time to learn how to study for classes and get adjusted to the volume of medical school.

First Year Second Semester

Begin learning how to take H & Ps in a standardized patient setting. Some schools may begin introducing OSCE (Objective Structured Clinical Examination) at this point.

Enjoy your last free summer vacation until your fourth year of medical school after Match and Graduation.

Second Year First Semester

Continue with OSCE's. Begin writing thorough SOAP notes after each encounter.

Stay focused in classes. No need for board preparation yet.

Second Year Second Semester

Formulate a study plan for your first round of national standardized written board exams. For competitive residency programs, it is more advantageous for DO students to take both.

Do NOT neglect your classes to take more time for board preparation. The material you learn in your courses is relevant for boards. If you are performing well in classes and have extra time set aside for board prep, by all means, study for both. However, sacrificing preparation for class exams when you are not performing well, only guarantees that your class grades will drop and does not necessarily mean you will perform any better on boards. In addition, students tend to have anywhere from 1-3 months of dedicated board study time after second year classes have ended and before they take there individually scheduled board exams. As long as you make good use of this time, students should not need to overlap studying for boards while still taking exams in second year classes.

**How you should study: Refer to chapter 13.

Start looking into elective rotations in specialties you may be interested in pursuing for third year.

Take your first round of board exams in the summer of your second year.

Third Year First Semester

Learn how to be professional, presentable, and comfortable out in the real world.

Start studying for shelf exams from the very start of each rotation. This will also help you for your second round of boards at the end of the year.

Perform at your best on each rotation, even if you do not plan on entering that specialty. It is useful to have many preceptors to ask for strong letters of recommendation. Multiple strong, diverse letters are better than multiple weak specialty-specific letters, so long as you have at least one or two strong specialty-specific letters, the others can typically be from any preceptor you want. It also helps your application/Dean's letter to have good evaluations from every preceptor with whom you rotated. This shows that you get along with everyone, no matter what specialty you are working in. You also might change your mind about what specialty you want to do later in third year, and at that time, it's nice to have a fall-back preceptor to write you that letter.

Ask your preceptor for the letter at the end of the rotation but understand that he/she may need a month or two. Avoid asking for letters of recommendation at the last minute. You can also let the preceptor know at the beginning of the rotation that you are interested in getting a strong letter of recommendation and that you will do the work that it takes to get it. This is best for when you know this specialty is what interests you.

Start working on a CV/Resume, and start thinking about your personal statement.

Third Year Second Semester

If you plan to audition at other programs, many of them will expect you to attach a CV/Resume and/or a small personal statement to your application, long before you ever begin your residency application in fourth year, so have these finalized, and proofread/edited by someone else if desired. These applications open up to medical students as early as December/January, and spots tend to fill up very quickly.

Take your second round of board exams, including your national standardized clinical patient encounter exam, in the summer of your third year.

**How you should study: Refer to chapter 13 again.

Fourth Year First Semester

Begin to audition in your specialty of choice at locations you may be interested in doing residency training. While you're on these auditions, show up early and stay late. Be kind to everyone and show enthusiasm. Make everyone know how easy and enjoyable it is to work with you, and this will help gain an interview at this program later.

Begin residency applications to programs/specialties of interest and submit in the Fall.

Fourth Year Second Semester

Begin your interview season. Interview invites can be sent out almost immediately after submitting your application, and the earliest interview dates are early October, and can go as late as late January/early February.

Match day in March. All your hard work pays off when you get your top choice specialty/program. The more work you put in, the less likely you are to have to Scramble/SOAP into a program that didn't fill it's spots (and that wasn't your top choice specialty/program).

Don't check out/get senioritis after Match day, **use the rest of your medical school education to get great training that will prepare you for your residency.** We recommend rotating through the intensive care unit as it prepares you for complex cases you may incur during your first few months of residency.

Graduation and celebration!

Chapter 13 Written Board Exams; How to Become a Professional Test Taker

There is no one way to study, however, it just seems to make inherent sense that the best way to get good at taking multiple choice question style exams is by doing lots of multiple choice practice questions. I mean, if you want to get good at kick-boxing, do you take up soccer, or would you just go to a kick-boxing class? Probably the latter. So, if you wanted to get really good at answering multiple choice questions, why would you spend time reading books or watching videos instead of answering practice questions? This news tends to come as a surprise to medical students who are used to tightly clutching their review books. Although these are good resources for learning, they lack something that only practice questions will give you. Practice questions will give you content review while also showing you **what** question writers like to ask about and **how** they like to ask about it. Practice tests will develop your speed, endurance, and testing strategy. The more questions you do, the more likely you are to have already seen the question once you are taking boards, and you will know the answer right away. We recommend doing THOUSANDS of multiple choice questions in preparation for the boards. This means completing multiple question banks and taking a wide variety of practice exams. Here are two reasons why you can forgo the review books and videos when it comes time for dedicated board study:

1) Although it's tempting for students to continue doing what they are used to doing in their first two years of medical school (powerpoints, reading books, watching lecture or mnemonic videos), board exams are a completely different challenge than the exams you are used to taking in medical school courses. First of all, up until this point you have probably never had to take an 8 hour exam on medical school level content, nor have you ever taken an exam that is all-inclusive of what you learned in the first two years of medical school. So, if you initially had two years to learn all the material for board exams, how the heck do you review it all in 2 months or less before you take the exam? How do you get thorough, effective content review if you don't have the time to look at everything you used the last two years? How do you build stamina and endurance to avoid fatigue when you've never taken an 8 hour exam at this level of content before? Well, if you do 5,000-10,000 questions or more, which is certainly possible in a 2-3 month period, you will have had multiple practice questions on nearly every subject you learned about in your first

two years, and you will have gotten the endurance training you need to sit for a long exam.

2) Also, dedicated board study time is a time for ACTIVE learning (i.e. answering questions and problem solving), and not PASSIVE learning (i.e. reading or watching videos). As a general rule, passive learning is solely informational input and no output, in other words, you read or watch something and you don't practice utilizing the information, which, when it comes to answering very difficult board exam questions, is almost as bad as never having learned the material in the first place. Active learning, on the other hand, demands that you use your brain to think and recruits your knowledge base to solve problems. This develops algorithmic thinking, process of elimination, and a strong general sense of good testing strategy. This is exactly the kind of training you need in order to do well on board exams. Your board exams will require you to think outside the box and connect dots that are not apparent if you haven't been trained to solve those types of problems. Just knowing the information does not mean you know how to apply it, and it is better to know a little bit about everything and know how to apply what you know than to know a lot about one thing from reading about it for 5 hours and never having practiced applying it.

So how to go about doing all of this:

1. Have a daily "question quota," or a specific number of questions that you need to finish each day in order to finish multiple question banks before you take your exam. Incorporate timed practice tests into the mix as well. This allows the questions to guide your studying (identifying your weak areas, etc.) and provides structure to your study schedule, rather than sifting through an endless amount of books, powerpoints, and videos and entering a downward spiral of informational overload and wondering what's important to learn/remember, which of course, we all know you don't have the time to do. The question quota model of studying is the most stress-free, effective, and structured model of board studying, and your back will no longer hurt because your 800 page book is no longer weighing down your backpack. All you'll need is your computer and Wifi.

2. Do these questions on a teaching style mode, that way you immediately review why you got the answer right/wrong and what the underlying explanation is. This is a way to learn as you go through the questions, so that if you get another question on the same topic, you can again practice applying what you just learned and build on your knowledge base. And for those who are still clinging to their study books for deeper explanations, if you were to take each explanation from every tutor mode question in just one or two question banks, you would have an 800 page book. So, why not just do the questions and read the explanations and save time?

3. Do these questions at random, because this is how the questions will show up on real exams. For example, you need to be able to go from answering a second order gastroenterology microbiology question to a third order cardiac

pharmacology question at the click of a button. This is easy if you studied this way, and even easier if you've already seen both questions in your question banks.

4. Do not worry about trying to know everything at the end of each question. Answer it, read the explanation, and if you can't find further understanding after a quick internet search, then just move on. If that concept was high-yield/important to know, then you will inevitably see that topic come up again the more questions you do. By that time you will understand it. Your priority is simply meeting your designated question quota every single day. Essentially, your goal is to volumize and expand your scope of knowledge and testing strategy in the short period of dedicated time you have to study while avoiding getting bogged down by tiny details that may or may not show up on the real exam. As we stated before, it is MUCH better to know a little bit about everything than a lot about one thing, and your dedicated study time to do so is unfortunately limited, so you need to be quick and effective with whatever you decide to utilize to learn.

Chapter 14   Writing a Great Personal Statement For Residency Applications

The trials and tribulations incurred during medical school culminate during one's 4th year when they need to go on their biggest interview of their life: their residency interview. But as with most interviews, one needs an excellent resume (CV) and cover letter to walk in the door.

Hence a student's "Personal Statement" is what completes the package that is presented to residency directors who choose your fate.

An advantage to this is that it provides an opportunity to personalize your application, which unfortunately can look very itemized during the application process.

In communication we are successful when we use the "Three E's." These stand for *Engage, Educate and Enlist*. You engage a person by garnering their attention, then once you have their attention you educate them, and once they are educated you can enlist them (such as rank me for your residency).

So what makes a good personal statement?

Length

The length of your personal statement should be approximately one page. This gives you 5-8 paragraphs to tell your story without boring one to death. You don't want to be too short and sweet but rather to the point and hammer your message home without getting into trouble saying too much later.

Open with a grab, but don't choke them…

The average person puts down an article, book, essay within the first sentence if it doesn't catch them. So avoid opening your personal statement with "*I've always wanted to be a doctor…*" Putting your future residency director to sleep seven words in prevents him from remembering your application and choosing you for his program.

So instead you should focus on a personal story that led to your resolve to dedicate your life to others. Examples of this include:

My decision to pursue medicine began when I came to the United States with my family to start a new life……

The art of medicine compels one to study the canvas before haphazardly wielding a paintbrush. I learned this when……

But don't be too flowery. Get to the point early on in your first paragraph on how life experiences affected your decision to pursue medicine and the specific specialty for which you're applying.

Which brings us to….

Know your specialty

If you are planning to pursue a career in Family Medicine, don't discuss how you want to become a "Jack of all Trades." This isn't what family medicine is about. Just as the specialty of surgery isn't all about "cutting." Let them know in your statement that you *get it* by saying something like…..

Understanding the wide range of pathologies that may affect a patient of any age is paramount to becoming an excellent family physician.

Being an advocate for my female patients and enabling them to bring life into this world attracted me to the field of obstetrics and gynecology.

Show you're a team player

The residency director, who's interviewing you, needs to know you play well with others. The team with which you will work includes senior residents, attendings, nurses, ancillary staff and administrators to name a few. So incorporate in your letter how you are cognizant of how a patient's success is dependent on a hospital's "team approach."

Avoid negativity

Avoid insulting other specialties or specialists…which may occur inadvertently when describing why you chose your specialty. For example, in one personal statement I edited, the student wrote, "*I didn't want to be a doctor who just cuts, so I chose primary care instead.*"

A better approach would be, "*I found being a front-line provider, making the initial decisions in a patient's care, to be exciting.*"

Do your research

Most students begin their personal statement at the end of their third year, when actually it's during your third year when you can gain much insight into how to write it. So questions you may want to ask your preceptor are:

How do you define family medicine (or the specific specialty)?

How did you come to decide to pursue medicine?

What do you look for in a personal statement?

If you could give me any advice on what to include in my personal statement what would that be?

Additionally, ask your clinical education department for resources or examples of good personal statements. Prior graduates who secured their top five choices may have offered their personal statements to the medical school for others to use as a guide.

Have a format

Even though personal statements vary in length, creativity, subject matter and prose, there is a general format most appear to follow.

Part 1 – your eye-catching opener that gives the program director a glimpse into your passion, personality, and plan (entering the field of ......).

Part 2 – a patient case or moment in your past that led you to forming this educated decision to pursue a specific specialty. Don't go into too many specifics regarding the patient due to HIPPA, and make sure your decision to pursue a particular field was not done on a whim or at the last minute before fourth year.

Part 3 – explain why you would be a good candidate for their residency program. What makes you a good student, doctor, leader, team player, educator (you will be teaching medical students) and person. Don't itemize every accomplishment on your CV, but highlight some of your finest accomplishments and strengths.

Part 4 – after you've engaged and educated the reader, you are ready to enlist them. The final portion of your personal statement reinforces why you are an excellent candidate for their program and how your goals are aligned with theirs in terms of providing good patient care, educating others, and giving back to your community. This is also where you can suggest what you are looking for in a residency program, such as one that offers research opportunities.

Remember to end the personal statement with a note of gratitude, such as, *"Thank you for considering my application to your residency program."* A piece of humble pie goes along way.

Have it edited

When you have completed your personal statement, make sure you have someone else read it and find any grammatical and spelling errors. Although most residency directors do not expect you to be a professional linguist, errors in one's statement may suggest that you are haphazard, inattentive, have a lack of care for details, or lazy.

So in summary, being given the opportunity to market yourself is a gift. So don't put it off until the last minute and pray one draft does the trick. Write this as it's the most important 500 – 800 words of your life....

Chapter 15 Interview Tips for Residency Programs

Thousands of medical students will be competing with you for a position in a coveted residency. But despite one's academic prowess, the interview could make or break an applicant.

Therefore, let's get you ready for the biggest job interview of your life.

Know your audience

Every residency program is different. And each one has defining elements. So don't make the assumption that all hospitals, doctors, staff and teaching programs are the same.

Do your research before your interview, and know inside and out what makes them tick.

- *The services they offer that other institutions don't*
- *The type of community they serve*
- *Current research studies*
- *What are they known to have excelled at or trail-blazed*

It might even help to read up on the program director and see what he/she published.

Why?? Because the first question they ask you is:

Why did you choose *our* residency?

Know the specialty you're applying for

This may seem like a no-brainer but many students will, when nerves take over, cite misconceptions or negative stereotypes of the field their entering.

For example one may cite during a surgical residency interview that they "Prefer cutting over figuring out what the patient has."

Or during a family medicine interview say, "I don't like working in the hospital," or "I would rather be a Jack-Of-All-Trades, than specializing in one subject."

These answers could make the interviewer cringe. So the following examples may be better statements:

Surgery - "I enjoy working with both my mind *and* my hands when it comes to the vast amounts of pathology one sees as a surgeon."

Family Medicine - "I enjoy working with the family as a unit and am excited to have the capability to treat those of *all* ages."

Internal Medicine - "I'm fascinated by the complexity of cases seen in internal medicine and how the history and physical exams skills we learned in medical school can be just as accurate as the most powerful imaging study used when determining what is wrong with a patient."

Pediatrics - "Children make me laugh and smile and to be able to do that *every* work day is a rarity in many professions and specialties."

Remember it's an *interview*

The reason why you are sitting before them is because they liked what they saw on paper but now they need to see you how you act, speak, and compose yourself in person. So the same rules apply.

- Thank them before and after the interview, using a handshake when appropriate
- Dress professionally, but comfortably so you appear comfortable and professional
- Avoid slang and overly wordy responses
- Keep giggles to a minimum, even if they make a funny joke
- Be respectful
- Be gracious to *everyone* with whom you come into contact with that day from the security guard to the program director to the parking attendant
- Be humble
- If a question seems random, and you don't know the answer, respond with, "That's a good question, let me give some thought into my answer before I respond," to provide you with some pause to collect your thoughts.

Why should they pick you?

Each program is being inundated with applications and your competition is fierce. However, don't let that over-intimidate you. The fact that you clutched an interview means you are already ahead of the pack. Now you need to convince them they made the right choice in choosing to interview *you.*

1. Remark how appreciative you are in them giving you the opportunity to interview for such a highly coveted position.
2. Highlight your strengths and how they can be of benefit to their residency
3. If you are multilingual, don't hold your tongue, let them know!
4. If you did an audition rotation there and worked well with the residency team (less transitioning needed) remind them of how well you all worked together
5. If your academics and board scores are strong it can enhance their test score average
6. Some may straight up ask what three things make *you* valuable for their residency program
7. You want to become apart of the community in which the residency resides and help continue their good work.

Many programs want to train those who will stay instate and provide much-needed care to their residents. If you do plan on living in the state in which you train, make sure you let them know!

Will they try to trip you up?

The short answer....No. Program directors don't have time to waste by choosing applicants and then scaring them off or tricking them into performing badly.

However, they are going to want to get to know *you.* Residents and their attendings are committed to working with each other anywhere from 3-5 years and your future boss wants to know if you can make the cut and work well with others. Don't be afraid to show some personality but remember to be brief and continue to allow them control of the interview.

So what are some sample questions?
You might be asked any of the following:

- Why did you choose our residency?
- What made you choose this specialty?
- How would you define our specialty?
- What do you like about our institution?
- What do you dislike about our program?

- What sub-specialty are you interested in?
- Where do you want to live once you graduate?
- Do you work well with others?
- Give me an example of when you had a conflict with a coworker and how did it get resolved.
- What are your strengths?
- What are your weaknesses?
- Tell me about your research.
- Tell me about your volunteer work.
- Tell me about your community service.
- Have you had any leadership roles?
- Briefly touch upon some of your academic challenges.
- What do you do for fun?
- What are your hobbies?
- How do you relieve stress?
- Do you have family and friends who support your career choice?
- Do you read books, and what book are you currently reading?
- Describe a challenging patient case you've come across.
- How would you approach a colleague who is abusing narcotics?
- Where do you see yourself in 5-10 years?
- Do you have any questions for me?

For the final question, refrain from asking the interviewer questions that are easily answered on their website or catalog. Use the opportunity to show off your interests whether it's regarding what research, community partnership, or teaching opportunities exist. You can also ask them what they like about the program, why they chose to teach there, and what they would like to see in terms of evolution and progress.

After the interview

You will thank them and shake their hand but when you return home send a thank you note for their time. Don't stress over how your interview went. Most likely you performed better than you thought. Moreover expect your skills to improve with each interview. Some suggest to leave your favorite picks to the end until you gained more practice, however, some may argue to not allow the interviewer to get "applicant fatigue" such that by the time they meet you they have made their choice.

Practice with classmates or faculty if you need and remember to prepare

Finally, realize that you have interacted with hundreds if not thousands of individuals in your lifetime whether they were students, patients or faculty and are *very* skilled at what you do. If not you wouldn't be about to graduate medical school.

Chapter 16 The Do's and Don'ts in Rotations

Prep for the patient types ahead of time. If you are taking care of a patient in liver failure, you can be sure your attending will ask you questions regarding anasarca and jaundice. Likewise if you are coverating a patient with renal issues you should be aware of what causes an anion gap acidosis.

Never be late, shoot for early unless you think that will bother your attending.

Ask your preceptor if you can bring your study materials so you can stay to study, this allows you to be onsite in case residents need help or there procedures to be seen.

For overnight shift, ensure all your prn orders are done for IV fluids, fluids, diet, and potassium to avoid extra calls when you can get some shut eye.

The following may seem like no brainers but you'd be surprised the mistakes you make when you're short on sleep…..

Avoid checking your cell phone every few minutes, especially during rounds.

Always have a pen, at least 3 in your pockets

Take the gum and pens out of your pocket before you wash your white coat

Don't steal food from the nursing lounge or hospital cafeteria

Don't try to out-talk the attending. Let them finish and listen intently.

When asked a question, never give a BS answer. If you don't know the answer, tell him/ her you will research it

Avoid flirting with the staff

Be aware of the jokes you tell and laughing as patients may be suffering in the next room.

After your first week into your rotation ask what your preceptor/attending how you can improve your performance.

The longer you pretend to know something you don't, the harder it is to admit it later when you really need to know. So ask a senior resident or student as soon as you realize you don't have the necessary answers.

Don't blow off the shelf exams as these can very easily become lower priority during a busy rotation.

Don't bad mouth any of your prior teachers or attendings.   Chances are they hang out on the weekend.

Absorb, absorb, absorb….the training you get during your rotations is some of the most valuable.

You only get to be a student once…..So if there is pathology to be seen, ask to see it. If a patient or attending says "No" that's ok. We're all told No in our careers, expect it sometimes.

When following up on hospital patients the next day, don't forget to "check under the sheet" as bedsores, rashes, cellulitis, or edema could be brewing.

Practice, practice, practice…and even if you think you have mastered a skill, do it again.

And one last piece of advice…..at some point in your medical school training you will doubt yourself or find yourself disliking medicine. That's completely normal. Years of schooling can wear you down. We all have felt that way because medical school is one of the most difficult academic, physical, mental and emotional paths one can take. So don't give up and always ask for help. You will need help and a faculty member or buddy to lean on. Nobody becomes a doctor doing it all alone, so don't feel forced to. We all relied on each other, our staff, our family and our patients to be able to reach our dream. You got this! Now go become a doctor!

Chapter 17 Medical Spanish Made Easy

We healthcare professionals work with thousands of patients a year, the majority of them bilingual. Many of them speak Spanish as their primary language, and the importance of our understanding their history is paramount. True we can have an interpreter in the room, but taking the time to learn key words and understand nuances in the Spanish language is vital for a strong doctor-patient relationship.

So why don't more healthcare providers learn Spanish?

There are a few reasons for this. Firstly, it can be time consuming. This chapter breaks it down into easy bite-size learning morsels but, it does take time, and many healthcare providers are short of it.

Secondly, many feel they have to reach 100% fluency or bust. Not true. As long as there is an interpreter in the room you can increase your fluency little by little without feeling you have to be 100% fluent from the get-go.

Thirdly, many healthcare providers do not want to feel like a "student" when compared to their patient. They fear it could diminish their stature when in fact that's not true. Patients appreciate your wanting to meet them halfway, and many find it endearing that their provider is human and still educating themselves.

Fourthly, healthcare workers fear when trying to speak Spanish they will say something wrong accidentally and insult the patient. This won't happen if you inform the patient that you are learning and a beginner in Medical Spanish. Rarely will you mispronounce a word that ends up being translated as an insult.

Finally, many feel that taking on a new language is too much to learn in such a short period of time. But many Spanish words have similar bases and meanings as English, hence you'll be surprised at how much you currently possess in terms of a baseline vocabulary. And to become fluent in Medical Spanish, one does not need to learn the entire language.

Before we get started, here are some helpful tips….

Your communication does not have to be always be in full complete sentences, hence if you cannot speak a compound sentence but know the noun and verb you wish to use, you can still communicate effectively.

Grammar will come with time, so don't get hung up on the conjugation of the verbs.

Patients have patience, and many will help you find the correct word if you're struggling..

Early on in your learning, rather than ask open-ended questions, convert the sentences to those that can be easily answered by a Yes/No.

If you do not know a word, reach for a word you do know and describe it as best you can.

For example, let's say you are trying to find the word for the test strips (*tiras*) used by a diabetic and his glucometer. You get stumped, so instead try describing the paper that goes into the machine for diabetes (*papel por la maquina de diabetes*). It's not perfect but you will convey your message and then you can later learn and practice the correct terminology.

Always have an interpreter in the room! Just because you are learning Medical Spanish does not mean you have to be on your own all the time.

Jump in....start practicing your Spanish, even if its one word a day.

It's OK to make mistakes. You will be corrected and the patient will find it endearing that you are going through the effort to communicate with them.

Basic Rules

To help you improve your pronunciation of the below terms follow these simple rules:

The "h" is silent. So "Hola" is pronounced "Ola".

The "j" sound will be similar to our "h." So "jabon" is pronounced "habon".

A "d" in between two vowels will be pronounced "th." So "nada" sounds like "natha."

The vowels "a", "e", "i", "o", and "u" are pronounced as the following:

"a" = "ah", as in *casa*

"e" = "eh" as in *hermano*

"i" = "eee" as in *mi amiga*

"o" = "oh" as in *hermano*

"u" = "ooooh" as in *fruta*

"Y" will sound similar to english as in "yes" but as a vowel will sound like "eee" as in *Maria y Julio*

Accents over the vowel implies you put the stress on the accented letter. So "¿Cómo está?," would be "¿**Có**mo es**tá**?"

"ll" in a word has a "y" sound

"rr" in a word will have a trilled sound

"ñ" in a word has a "nyeh" sound.

If at the start of a word "v" sounds like "b". In the middle of the word "b" and "v" sound similar to each other, with "v" being a soft "v" so soft it can sound like a "b".

"You"

When we address an older individual or someone of respect we use Usted (pr. oooo-sted), with most verbs ending in a vowel. The familiar, informal, address is tú (pr. too), in which we end the verb with an "s". I would suggest always beginning the relationship using the formal, Ud., address, using the informal only in children and in those who allow you to, or are of the same rank and age.

Example: How are you? (formal)   *¿Cómo está Ud.?*

How are you? (informal)   *¿Cómo estás tú?*

Now in conversation, we sometimes do not use the specific pronoun "you", so commonly you will say *¿Cómo está?* or *¿Cómo estás?*.

Feminine Vs. Masculine

Nouns that begin in "La" signify female, hence when an adjective is used next to it, it will convert, usually changing the last letter to "a".

So with *la ropa* (the clothes), if we need to describe them as red *(rojo)* we would say *la ropa roj***a**.

Nouns that begin in "El" signify male, hence when an adjective is used next to it it will convert, usually changing the last letter to "o".
So with *el gato* (the cat), if we need to describe it as white (*blanca*), we would say *el gato blanc***o**.

Introductions and Establishing Rapport

ENGLISH	SPANISH
Pleased to meet you	Mucho Gusto
Hello	Hola
How are you?	¿Cómo está (formal)?
What is your name?	¿Cómo se llama?
How old are you?	¿Cuántos años tiene Ud.?
Goodbye	Adiós
See you later	Hasta Luego
Thank you	Gracias
You're welcome	De nada
Likewise (equally)	Igualmente

Introductions and Establishing Rapport Con't

ENGLISH	SPANISH
My name is....	Me llamo....
I am....	Soy....
This is (if assistant present)...	Este (esta) es....
I am the doctor	Soy el médico
I am the nurse	Soy la enfermera
I am the nurse practitioner	Soy la enfermera especialista
I am the physician assistant	Soy el asociado médico
I am the dentist	Soy el dentista
I am the physical therapist	Soy el fisioterapueta

Introductions and Establishing Rapport Con't

ENGLISH	SPANISH
Are you comfortable?	¿Está cómodo?
I'm going to wash my hands	Voy a lavarme las manos
May I have a seat?	¿Puedo tener un asiento? Or ¿Puedo sentarme aquí?

Chief Complaint and History of Present Illness

ENGLISH	SPANISH
Why are you here?	¿Por que estas (or esta) aqui?
What is the problem?	¿Cual es el problema?
What's going on?	¿Qué Pasa (not very formal)?
What's going on?	¿Qué Pasó?
Where is the pain?	¿Donde está es el dolor?
Does the pain move?	¿Se mueve el dolor?
What makes it worse?	¿Lo que lo hace peor?
What makes it better?	¿Lo que lo hace mejor?
When did it start?	¿Cuando empezá?
What have you done that helps?	¿Qué has hecho ayudó?

CC and HPI Con't

ENGLISH	SPANISH
Did it start suddenly	¿Empezó de repente?
Did it start gradually	¿Empezó gradualmente?
Describe the pain	Describa el dolor.
How bad is the pain	¿Qué tan grave es el dolor?
On a scale of 1 to 10, how strong is the pain	¿En una escala de 1 a 10, qué tan fuerte es el dolor?
Is it continuous	¿Es continua?
Once in a while	De vez en cuando
Comes in waves	Viene en oleadas

Associated Symptoms

ENGLISH	SPANISH
Do you have....	¿Tiene (s)....
....nausea	....nausea
....vomiting	....vomitos
....diarrhea	....diarrea
....pain	....dolor
....fever	....calentura/fiebre
....rash	....erupción/picadura
....dizziness?	....mareo/mareada?

Associated Symptoms Con't.

ENGLISH	SPANISH
Are you....	¿Estás....
....Tired	....Cansado
....Weak	....Débil
....Constipated	....Estreñido/constipado
....Sad	....Triste
....Thirsty	....Sed/sediento
....Anxious	....Ansioso
....Depressed	....Deprimido
....Nervous?	....Nervioso?

Associated Symptoms Con't

ENGLISH	SPANISH
Do you have….	¿Tiene ….
….cough	….tos
….sneezing	….estornudos
….discharge	….flujo
….mucous	….moco
….pus	….pus
….burning with urination	….ardor al orinar
….blood in your stool (excremento)	….sangre en su popo
Have you travelled recently?	¿Has viajado recientemente?
Are your vaccines up to date?	Están sus vacunas al día?

Past Medical History

ENGLISH	SPANISH
Have you had problems with your....	¿Ha tenido problemas con su....
....health	....salud
....thyroid	....tiroides
....heart	....corazón
....lungs	....pulmones
....liver	....higado
....kidneys	....riñones
....intestines	....intestinos
....blood?	....sangre?

PMH Con't

ENGLISH	SPANISH
Have you had….	¿Ha tenido
….Diabetes	…Diabetes
….High Blood Pressure	….Alta presión
….Asthma	….Asma
….Cancer	….Cáncer
….High Cholesterol	….Colesterol alto
….Stroke cerebro/infarto/embolia	….Derrame de
….Heart Attack?	….Ataque al corazón?

PMH Con't

ENGLISH	SPANISH
Have you had….	¿Ha tenido….
….Urinary tract infection	….Infección de orina
….Gout	….Gota
….Weight loss	…. Pérdida de peso
….Hepatitis	….Hepatitis
…Arthritis	….Artritis
….Hospitalizations	….Hospitalizaciónes
….Operations	….Operaciónes
….Accidents	…. Accidentes
….Injuries	….Lesiones
….Wounds	….Heridas
….Sexually Transmitted Illnesses	….Enfermedades de transmisión sexual

OB/GYN History

ENGLISH	SPANISH
Period	Regla (período)
When was your last menstrual period (LMP)?	¿Cuándo fue su última regla?
Are your periods regular?	¿Son sus reglas regulares?
How heavy do you bleed?	¿Qué tan fuerte sangra?
How many tampons or pads do you use a day?	¿Cuántos tampones o almohadillas usa al día?
Are you currently pregnant?	¿Está embarazada actualmente?
How many pregnancies have you had?	¿Cuántos embarazos ha tenido?
Was the birth vaginal or c-section?	¿Fue el parto vaginal o cesárea?
Have you lost any pregnancies?	¿Ha perdido algún embarazo?

OB/Gyn History con't

ENGLISH	SPANISH
Can you feel the baby kick?	¿Puede sentir la patada del bebé?
Do you have any abnormal bleeding?	¿Tiene algún sangrado anormal?
Do you have any vaginal discharge?	¿Tiene flujo vaginal?
What color is it?	¿De qué color es?
Does it have an odor?	¿Tiene un olor?

Medications And Allergies

ENGLISH	SPANISH
What medications are you taking?	¿Qué medicinas está tomando?
How much are you taking?	¿Cuantos está tomando?
How many times a day?	¿Cuántas veces al día?
Do you have allergies to some medications?	¿Tiene alergia a algún medicamento?
What happens when you take it?	¿Que pasa cuando lo toma?
....Rash?	….Erupción/picadura?
…Difficulty breathing?	Dificultad para respirar/Falta respirar?
Nothing has changed since your last visit?	¿Nada ha cambiado desde su última visita?

Family History

ENGLISH	SPANISH
Are there any medical problems with…	¿Hay alguna problemas médicos con…
….your mother	….su madre
….your father	….su padre
….your brothers and sisters	….sus hermanos
….your grandparents	….sus abuelos
….your aunts/uncles?	….sus tías/tíos?
Are your parents still alive?	¿Estan vivos de sus padres?
What did he die of?	¿De qué murio de?
I'm sorry/I'm sorry to hear that	Lo siento/Siento escuchar eso
At what age?	¿A qué edad?
What happened?	¿Qué pasó?

Social History

ENGLISH	SPANISH
Do you smoke?	¿Fuma Ud.?
How much do you smoke?	¿Cuánto fuma Ud.?
Do you vape?	¿Vape?
Do you use marijuana?	¿Usa marihuana?
Do you use recreational drugs?	¿Usa drogas recreativas?
Do you drink alcohol?	¿Bebe alcohol?
How much do you drink?	¿Cuánto bebe?

CAGE Questions

Have you ever felt the need to *Cut* back?

¿Alguna vez has sentido la necesidad de recortar?

Do you get *Annoyed* when someone criticizes your drinking?

¿Te molesta cuando alguien critica tu forma de beber?

Have you ever felt *Guilty* about your drinking?

¿Alguna vez te has sentido culpable por beber?

Have you ever needed to drink first thing in the morning?

¿Alguna vez has necesitado beber a primera hora de la mañana?

(Eye-opener)

Work History

ENGLISH	SPANISH

What do you do for work?　　　　　¿En qué trabaja?

Are you **able to work** with your current medical issue?
　　　　　　　¿**Puedes trabajar** con tu problema Médico actual?

How many hours a day do you work?　　¿Cuántas horas al día trabajas?

How many days a week do you work?　　¿Cuántos días a la semana trabaja?

Do you **need a work note** for some time off?
　　　　　　　¿**Necesitas una nota** de trabajo por un tiempo libre?

Sexual History

ENGLISH	SPANISH
Are you sexually active?	¿Son sexualmente activos?
Are you married?	¿Esta casada?
Are you in a monogamous relationship?	¿Estás en una relación monógama?
Do you have sex with men, women, or both?	¿Tiene relaciones sexuales con hombres, mujeres o ambos?
Have you had sex without protection?	¿Ha tenido relaciones sexuales sin protección?
Has the sex you've had been consensual?	¿Tiene el sexo que has tenido consensuado?
Have you felt safe in your relationship?	¿Se siente seguro en su relación?
Would you like to be tested for STI's?	¿Le gustaría ser examinado para las ITS (infecciones sexuales)?

Simple Commands

ENGLISH	SPANISH
Please….	Por favor….
Relax	Relaje
Look straight	Mire derecho
Follow the light	Siga (Sigue) la luz
Follow my finger	Siga (Sigue) mi dedo
Open your mouth	Abre la boca
Stick out your tongue	Saca la lengua
Swallow	Trague

Simple Commands Con't

ENGLISH	SPANISH
Bend your wrist	Doble la muñeca
Bend your knee	Doble el rodillo
Bend your ankle	Doble el tobillo
Can you feel this?	¿Puede sentir esto?
Does this hurt?	Duele esto/se duele?
Put your hands out	Pone sus manos
Are you numb?	¿Esta insensibilizar/durmiendo?

Simple Commands Con't

ENGLISH	SPANISH
Breathe deeply	Respire profundo/profundamente
Don't breathe	No respire
Hold your breath	Contenga la respiración/no respire
Lift your arm	Levante el brazo
Lift your leg	Levante la pierna
Squeeze my hand	Apriete la mano

Simple Commands Con't

ENGLISH	SPANISH
Lie down	Acuestase
Get up	Levante
Turn	Vuelta
Bend	Doble
Look	Mire
Listen	Eschuche
Undress	Desnude
Dress	Vestase

Parts of the Body

Note: I've included the definite articles in Spanish to help identify masculine or feminine.

Head and Neck

ENGLISH	**SPANISH**
(The) head	La cabeza
Hair	El pelo
Eyes	Los ojos
Ears (inner/outer)	Los oídos/orejas
Nose	La nariz
Mouth	La boca
Teeth	Los dientes
Tongue	La lengua

Head and Neck Con't

ENGLISH	SPANISH
(The) neck	El Cuello
Chin	La Barbilla
Beard	La Barba
Lymph Nodes	Los Ganglios linfaticos
Carotid	La Carotída
Throat	La Garganta
Larynx	La Laringe

The Chest

ENGLISH	SPANISH
(The) Chest	El Pecho
Heart	El Corazón
Lungs	Los Pulmones
Ribs	Las Costillas
Sternum	El Esternón
Diaphragm	El Diafragma
Breasts	Los Senos
Nipples	Los Pezones
Skin	La Piel

Abdomen

ENGLISH	SPANISH
(The) Stomach	El Estómago
Spleen	El Bazo
Belly button (umbilicus)	El Ombligo
Pancreas	El Pancreas
Liver	El Higado
Gallbladder	La Vesícula (de biliar)
Intestines (small/large)	Los Intestinos (delgado/grueso)
Colon	El Colón
Rectum	El Recto
Kidney	El Riñon

Genitourinary

ENGLISH	SPANISH
(The) Bladder	La vejiga
Uterus	La matriz/utero
Cervix	La boca de matriz
Ovary	El ovario
Testicle	El testículo
Penis	El pene
Prostate	La próstata
Vagina	La vagina
Fallopian tube	El tubo de ovario/trompa de Falopio

Upper Extremity

ENGLISH	SPANISH
(The) Hand	La mano
Finger	El dedo
Wrist	La muñeca
Arm	El brazo
Elbow	El codo
Shoulder	El hombro
Clavicle	La clavícula

Lower Extremity

ENGLISH	SPANISH
(The) Toe	El dedo (del pie)
Foot	El pie
Ankle	El tobillo
Leg	La pierna
Knee	La rodilla
Hip	La cadera
Pelvis	La pelvis

Musculoskeletal (including spine)

ENGLISH	**SPANISH**
(The) Back	La espalda
Muscles	Los músculos
Tendons	Los tendones
Ligaments	Los ligamentos
Bones	Los huesos
Fracture	La fractura
Broken	Roto
Broken bone	El roto hueso/hueso fracturado
Sprain	Esguince
Strain	Tensión

Musculoskeletal Con't

ENGLISH	SPANISH
Cramps	Calambres
Spasms	Espasmos
(The) Cervical neck	El cuello cervical
Thoracic	Torácica
Lumbar spine	Espina lumbar
Low back	Espalda baja
Vertebrae	Las vertebras
Discs	Los discos
Sciatica	Ciatica

Industry Terms

ENGLISH	SPANISH
(The) hospital	El hospital
Office/clinic	La oficina/clinica
Waiting Room	La sala de espera
Bathroom	El baño
Room	El cuarto
Bed	La cama
Exam table	La mesa de examen
Laboratory	El laboratorio
Insurance	Seguro/aseguranza

Industry Terms Con't

ENGLISH	SPANISH
(The) Prescription	La receta
Pill	La pastilla
Milligrams	Miligramos
Sample	La muestra
Referral/recommendation	La recomendación
Specialist	La especialista
Appointment	La cita
Visit	La visita

Industry Terms Con't

ENGLISH	SPANISH
Take the medicine	Tome la medicina
Two times a day	Dos veces al día
A half a tablet/pill	Un medio una piladora/pasilla
Take it with food	Tomarlo con comida
Drink plenty of water	Tome mucha agua
Do not mix with alcohol	No se mezclan con alcohol
Do not eat past midnight	No coma nada después de medianoche
Do you understand?	¿Lo entiendes/Entiende Ud.?
Any questions?	¿Alguna pregunta/Preguntas?

Days of the Week

ENGLISH	SPANISH
Monday	Lunes
Tuesday	Martes
Wednesday	Miércoles
Thursday	Jueves
Friday	Viernes
Saturday	Sábado
Sunday	Domingo

Months

ENGLISH	SPANISH
January	Enero
February	Febrero
March	Marzo
April	Abril
May	Mayo
June	Junio

Months con't

ENGLISH	SPANISH
July	Julio
August	Agosto
September	Septiembre
October	Octubre
November	Noviembre
December	Diciembre

Numbers

ENGLISH	SPANISH
One	Uno
Two	Dos
Three	Tres
Four	Quatro
Five	Cinco
Six	Seis
Seven	Siete
Eight	Ocho
Nine	Nueve
Ten	Diez

Numbers Con't

ENGLISH	SPANISH
Twenty	Veinte
Thirty	Treinta
Forty	Cuarenta
Fifty	Cinquenta
Sixty	Sesenta
Seventy	Setenta
Eighty	Ochenta
Ninety	Noventa
One hundred	Cien

Numbers Con't

ENGLISH	SPANISH
200	Doscientos
250	Doscientos cincuenta
500	Quinientos
1000	Un mil
2000	Dos mil
One million	Un millon
The pill is 500 mg	La pastilla es de quinientos miligramos

Safe Words
(if having difficulty understanding the patient)

I am practicing my Spanish   Estoy practicando mi español

Thank you for your patience (understanding)

                    Gracias por su paciencia(comprension)

More slowly please   Más lentamente/despacio por favor

One more time   Una vez más

Please repeat   Por favor, repitelo

Hypertension Common Terms

High blood pressure	Alta presión
Check your pressure	Cheque su presión
Heart	Corazón
Chest pain	Dolor de pecho
Shortness of breath (SOB)	Falta respirar
Take the medicine	Tome las medicinas
Swollen?	¿Hinchado?
Dizzy?	¿Mareada/Mareo?

Diabetes Common Terms

ENGLISH	SPANISH
Sugar	Azucar
Check sugar	Cheque su azúcar
Glucometer	Glucómetro
Needles	Agujas
Insulin	Insulina
Test Strips	Tiras reactivas glucosa
In the morning	En la mañana
Without eating	Sin comer
After eating	Después de comer
Blurry vision	Visión borrosa
Urinate frequently	Orinar con frecuencia/frequentemente
Bread, rice, treats, fruits have sugar azucar	Pan, arroz, dulces, frutas tiene
Check your feet daily	Revisa sus pies diariamente

Basic History and Physical Practice

Thank them for waiting

> *Gracias a su espera/por su esperar/por esperar*

Shake their hand and say

> *Mucho Gusto* (much pleased)

Introduce yourself

> *Me llamo....* (or) *Soy....*

Ask how they would like to be addressed

> *¿Como se llama?*

Excuse yourself to go to wash your hands (if not already done)

> *Perdon, voy a lavarme las manos.*

Return and ask if you can sit down

> *¿Puedo sentarme?*

What brings you in today?

> *¿Cual es el problema?*
> **or**
> *¿Porque esta aqui?*

How old are you?

¿Cuantos anos Ud. tiene?

A physical exam? Very good!

¿Un Examen físico? ¡Muy bien!

When was your last exam?

¿Su última examen?

Was everything normal?

¿Era todo normal?

How do you feel?

¿Cómo se siente?

Do you have any medical problems?

¿Tienes algun problema medico?
or
¿Problemas medicos?

….Diabetes

….Cancer

….Asma (asthma)

….Ataque al corazón (heart attack)

….Derrame cerebral or émbolo de cerebro
(stroke)

....Tiroides (thyroid)?

For how long?

Por cuánto tiempo?

Are there medical problems in your family?

¿Hay problemas médicos en su familia?
Or
¿Y su familia?

....Father

.... Padre

....Mother

....Madre

....Grandparents

....Abuelos

....Siblings

....Hermanos

All are good?

¿Todos estan bien?

He died?

¿Se murio?

I'm sorry

Lo Siento

Have you had any operations?

¿Ha tenido alguna operación?
Or
¿Operaciones?

When?

¿Cuando?

Why?

¿Porque?

Any accidents?

¿Accidentes?

Are you taking any medications?

¿Está tomando alguna medicación?
or
¿Su medicinas?

For what condition?

¿Para que condición?
or
¿Porque?

How much are you taking?

¿Cuanto está tomando?
or
¿Cuanto?

Do you have any allergies to medications?

¿Ud. tiene alguna alergia a los medicamentos?
or
¿Alergias?

What happens?

¿Qué pasa?

What happened?

¿Qué pasó?

Operations?

¿Operaciones?

Accidents?

¿Accidentes?

Do you smoke?

¿Fuma Ud? ¿Tabaco? ¿Marihuana? ¿Vape?

Do you drink alcohol?

¿Bebe alcohol?

Do you use drugs?

¿Usa drogas?

Are you having unprotected sex?

¿Estas teniendo relaciones sexuales sin Protección?

With men, women or both?

¿Con hombres, mujeres or ambos?

Have you ever had an STI?

¿Infecciones?
or

¿Ha tenido una infección de transmisión sexual?

Are you married?

¿Esta casada(o)?

Have you travelled recently?

¿Has viajado recientemente?
or
¿Viaje recientemente? Donde (where)?

Have you had all your vaccines?

Ha tenido todas su vacunas?

As you go through the physical mention each body to practice your vocabulary. Additionally you can ask some Review of Systems while examining them by asking them if they have problems with (*problemas con*....)

Relax

Relaje

Let's begin the exam

Comencemos el examen
or
Vamos a empezar (let's begin)

Head

Cabeza

Eyes

Ojos

Ears

oídos

Mouth

Boca

Open your mouth

Abre la boca

Stick out your tongue

Saca la lengua

Neck

Cuello

Thyroid

Tiroides

Swallow

Trague

Chest

Pecho

Lower the gown (to listen to heart and lung sounds)

Baje el vestido

Lungs

Pulmones

Breath deeply

Respire profundo

Heart

Corazón

Breath normally

Respire normal

Lie back

Acuestase

Abdomen

Abdomen

Stomach

Estomago

Bend your knees (helps relax the abdomen when lying down)

Doble las rodillas

Sit up

Levantase

Back

Espalda

Bend

Doble

Spasms?

¿Espasmos?

Your exam today is normal

Su examen de hoy es normal ....

o

Todos normal...

Except for spasms in the back

....salvo (excepto) espasmos en la espalda

Would you like therapy or OMM?

¿Quiere terapia o manipulación Osteopática?

Return in one week, month, or year

Regrese en una semana, mes, (or) año

Until next time!

¡Hasta Luego!

Now this was a very basic physical but with practice the words will come more naturally and you can expand on this as the patient has more issues.

ENGLISH-SPANISH MEDICAL TERM DICTIONARY

ENGLISH	SPANISH

A

A	Un/una
Abnormal	Anormal
Accidents	Accidentes
Active	Activos
After	Después
Age	Edad
AIDS	SIDA
Alcohol	Alcohol
Allergy	Alergia
Alive	Viva
Also	También
Anemia	Anemia
Ankle	Tobillo
Annoy	Molestar
Anxiety	Ansiedad
Anxious	Ansioso
Any	Alguna
April	Abril
Appointment	Cita
Arm	Brazo
Arthritis	Artritis
Assessment	Evaluación
Assistive device	Dispositivo de asistencia
Asthma	Asma
At	A
Attack	Ataque
August	Agosto
Aunt	Tía

B

Baby	Bebé

Back	Espalda
Bacteria	Bacteria
Bad	Mal/ grave
Balance	Equilibrar
Bath	Bañera
Bathroom	Baño
Beard	Barba
Because	Porque
Bed	Cama
Before	Antes de
Begin	Empezar
Bend	Doblar
Better	Mejor
Birth	Parto/nacimiento
Black	Negro
Bladder	Vejiga
Blood	Sangre
Blood Pressure	Presión sanguínea
Blue	Azul
Bone	Hueso
Born	Nacido
Both	Ambos
Bother	Molestar
Breathe	Respirar
Breasts	Senos/pechos
Broken	Roto
Broken bone	El roto hueso/hueso fracturado
Bronchitis	Bronquitis
Brother	Hermano
Brown	Marrón/moreno/cafe
Bursh	Cepillar
Burn (none)	Quemadura
Burn (verb)	Quemar/arder

C

Call	Llama
Can (verb)	Poder
Cancer	Cáncer
Cane	Caña/bastón
Carotid	Carotída
Cervical Neck	Cuello cervical
Cervical Spine	Columna cervical/espina cervical
Cervix	Boca de la matriz
Cesarean	Cesárea
Chair	Silla
Change	Cambiar
Check (verb)	Chequear/comprobar/verificar/revisar
Chest	Pecho

Chew	Masticar
Children	Niños
Chin	Barbilla
Cholesterol	Colesterol
Clavicle	Clavícula
Clinic	Clinica
Close (verb)	Cerrar
Closed	Cerrado
Cold (virus)	Gripa
Cold (temperature)	Frío
Colon	Colón
Color	Color
Come	Venir
Comfortable	Cómodo
Condom	Condón
Congestion	Congestión
Consensual	Consensuado
Constipated	Constipado/estreñido
Continuous	Continua
Cough	Tos
Cousin	Primo
Cramps	Calambres
Currently	Actualmente

D

Daily	Diario/diariamente
Daughter	Hija
Day	Día
Dead	Muerto
December	Diciembre
Deep	Profundo
Deeply	Profundamente
Dental Floss	Hilo dental
Dentist	Dentista
Depressed	Deprimido
Describe	Describir
Diabetes	Diabetes
Diagnosis	Diagnóstico
Diaphragm	Diafragma
Diarrhea	Diarrea
Die	Morir
Difficulty/lack	Dificultad/falta
Discharge	Flujo/desecho
Discs	Discos
Dizziness	Mareo/mareada
Doctor	Médico/doctor
Down	Abajo
Drink	Beber/tomar

Dress (verb)	Vestir
Drugs	Drogas

E

Ear (inner)	oído
Ear (outer)	Oreja
Easy	Facíl
Eat	Comer
Elbow	Codo
English	Inglés
Exam	Examen
Exam table	Mesa de examen
Examine	Examinar
Exercise	Ejercicio
Experience	Experiencia
Eye	Ojo

F

Fallopian tube	El tubo de ovario/trompa de Falopio
Father	Padre
February	Febrero
Feel	Sentir
Fever	Fiebre/calentura
Finger	Dedo
First	Primera
Flu	Gripe/influenza
Follow	Seguir
Food	Comida
Foot	Pie
For	Por/Para
Fracture	Fractura
Frequently	Frecuentemente
Free (liberated)/(no cost)	Libre/gratis
Friday	Viernes

G

Gallbladder	Vesícula de biliar
Glucometer	Glucómetro
Goals	Metas
Good	Bueno/bien
Goodbye	Adiós
Gout	Gota
Guilty	Culpable
Gradually	Gradualmente
Green	Verde
Grandparent	Abuelo

H

Hair	Pelo
Hand	Mano
Happen	Pasar
Have	Tener
Head	Cabeza
Health	Salud
Hear	Escuchar
Heart	Corazón
Heart Attack	Ataque al corazón
Hello	Hola
Help (noun)	Ayuda
Help (verb)	Ayudar
Hepatitis	Hepatitis
Here	Aquí
High	Alto
High Blood Pressure	Alta Presión
High Cholesterol	Colesterol alto
Hip	Cadera
HIV	VIH
Hold	Contener/sostener
Home	Casa
Hospital	Hospital
Hospitalizations	Hospitalizaciónes
Hot	Caliente/calor
Hour	Hora
How	¿Cómo?
How are you?	¿Cómo está?
How much?	¿Cuántos?

I

I am	Soy
I am sorry	Lo siento
Illnesses	Enfermedades
In	En
Infection	Infección
Inflamed	Inflamado
Injuries	Lesiones
Insurance	Seguro/aseguranza
Insulin	Insulina
Intestines	Intestinos
Is	Es

J

January	Enero
Jaundice	Ictericia
June	Junio
July	Julio

K

Kick	Patada
Kidney	Riñon
Knee	Rodillo

L

Laboratory	Laboratorio
Large intestine	Intestino grueso
Larynx	Laringe
Last	Última
Later	Luego
Left	Izquierda
Leg	Pierna
Lie down	Acostar
Lift	Levantar
Ligaments	Ligamentos
Light	Luz
Like (verb)	Gustar
Like (similar)	Como
Likewise	Igualmente
Listen	Escuchar
Live	Vivir
Liver	Higado
Look	Mirar
Lose	Perder
Low	Bajo
Low back	Espalda baja
Lumbar Spine	Espina lumbar
Lungs	Pulmones
Lymph nodes	Ganglios linfáticos

M

Machine	Máquina
Make	Hacer
Man	Hombre
March	Marzo
Marijuana	Marijuana/marihuana
Married	Casada
May	Mayo
Medications	Medicinas/medicamentos
Midnight	Medianoche
Milligrams	Miligramos
Mix	Mezclar
Monday	Lunes
Monogamous	Monógama
More	Más
Morning	Mañana

Mother	Madre
Mouth	Boca
Move	Mover
Movement	Movimiento
Much	Mucho
Mucous	Moco
Muscles	Músculos
My	Mi

N

Name	Nombre
Nausea	Nausea
Neck	Cuello
Need	Necesitar
Needles	Agujas
Nervous	Nervioso
Next	Próxima
Nipples	Pezones
Nose	Nariz
Note	Nota
Nothing	Nada
November	Noviembre
Numb	Durmiendo/insensibilidad/entumecimiento
Nurse	Enfermera
Nurse practitioner	Enfermera especialista

O

October	Octubre
Odor	Olor
Of	De
Office	Oficina
Open (ver)	Abrir
Open (adj)	Abierto
Operations	Operaciónes
Or	O
Orange	Naranja
Ovary	Ovario

P

Pads	Almohadillas
Pain	Dolor
Pale	Pálido
Pancreas	Pancreas
Patience	Paciencia
Pelvis	Pelvis
Penis	Pene
Period	Regla (período)
Physical therapist	Fisioterapueta

Physician assistant	Asistente/asociado médico
Pill	Pastilla
Pink	Rosado
Plan	Plan
Please	Por favor
Pleased to meet you	Mucho gusto
Point (verb)	Apuntar
Pollen	Pólen
Poop	Popo/excremento
Practice	Practicar
Pregnancy	Embarazo
Pregnant	Embarazada
Prescription	Receta
Pressure	Presión
Problem	Problema
Program	Programa
Prostate	Próstata
Protection	Protección
Put	Poner
Purple	Morado
Pus	Pus

Q

Question	Pregunta

R

Raise	Levantar/elevar
Rash	Erupción/picadura
Recently	Recientemente
Recreational	Recreativas
Recto	Rectum
Red	Rojo
Referral/recommendation	Recomendación
Regular	Regular
Relationship	Relación
Relax	Relaje
Repeat	Repetir
Respiration	Respiración
Return	Regresar
Ribs	Costillas
Right	Derecha
Room	Cuarto

S

Sad	Triste
Sample	Muestra
Saturday	Sábado
Scale	Escala

Sciatica	Ciática
Seat	Asiento
September	Septiembre
Sex	Sexo
Sexual	Sexual
Shoulder	Hombro
Show (verb)	Mostrar
Shower	Ducha
Since	Desde
Sister	Hermana
Skin	Piel
Slowly	Despacio/lentamente
Small intestine	Intestino delgado
Smoke	Fumar
Sneezing	Estornudos
Some	Algunos
Someone	Alguien
Son	Hijo
Spanish	Español
Spasms	Espasmos
Specialist	Especialista
Spleen	Bazo
Sprain	Esguince
Squeeze	Apretar
Sternum	Esternón
Stomach	Estómago
Stop	Parar/detener
Stick out	Sacar
Stool (poop)	Popo/excremento
Stool/defecate (verb)	Defecar
Straight	Derecho
Straighten	Enderezar
Strain	Tensión
Strength	Fuerza
Stretch	Estirar
Strong	Fuerte
Stroke	Derrame de cerebro/infarto/embolia
Suddenly	De repente
Sugar	Azucar
Sunday	Domingo
Swallow	Tragar
Swelling	Hinchazón
Swollen	Hinchado

T

Take (as in medicine)	Tomar
Tampons	Tampones
Teeth	Dientes

Test	Examen
Test strips	Tiras reactivas glucosa
Testicle	Tesículo
Thank you	Gracias
That	Ese
Therapist	Terapista
There	Ahí, allí
There is	Hay
Thing	Cosa
Thirsty	Sed/sediento
This	Esta
Thoracic	Torácica
Throat	Garganta
Thursday	Jueves
Thyroid	Tiroides
Time	Vez/tiempo
Tired	Cansado
Toe	Dedo (del pie)
Tomorrow	Mañana
Tongue	Lengua
Transmission	Transmisión
Travel	Viajar
Treatment plan	Plan de tratamiento
Tuesday	Martes
Turn	Volver/girar

U

Uncle	Tío
Understand	Entender
Undress	Desnudar
Until	Hasta
Up	Arriba
Urine	Orina
Urinate	Orinar
Use	Usar
Uterus	Matrix/utero

V

Vaccines	Vacunas
Vagina	Vagina
Vaginal	Vaginal
Vape	Vape
Vertebrae	Vertebras
Virus	Virus
Visit	Visita
Vision	Visión
Vomit	Vómito

W

Waiting room	Sala de espera
Walk	Caminar
Wash	Lavar
Water	Agua
Wave	Ola/oleada
Weak	Débil
Wednesday	Miércoles
Week	Semana
Weight	Peso
What	¿Qué?
Wheelchair	Silla de ruedas
When	¿Cuando?
Where	¿Donde?
Which	¿Cuál?
White	Blanco
Why	¿Por qué?
With	Con
Without	Sin
Woman	Mujer
Work	Trabaja
Worse	Peor
Wound	Herida
Wrist	Muñeca

X

X-ray	Radiografía

Y

Year	Año
Yellow	Amarillo
Your (informal)	Tu
Your (formal)	Su
You're Welcome	De nada

Z

Zoonotic disease	Enfermedad zoonótica